Hummingbirds and Hyenas

HUMMINGBIRDS
AND
HYENAS

Edward Pearce

faber and faber
LONDON · BOSTON

First published in 1985
by Faber and Faber Limited
3 Queen Square London WC1N 3AU

Photoset and printed in Great Britain by
Redwood Burn Limited, Trowbridge, Wiltshire
and bound by Pegasus Bookbinding, Melksham, Wiltshire

The lines quoted on p. 60 are taken from poem no. 23 'Crossing alone the night'
by A.E. Housman and reproduced by permission of the Society of Authors as
the literary representative of the Estate of A.E. Housman and Jonathan Cape
Ltd., publishers of A.E. Housman's *Collected Poems*.

British Library Cataloguing in Publication Data

Pearce, Edward
Hummingbirds and Hyenas.
1.   Great Britain. *Parliament. House of Commons*
2.   Legislators – Great Britain
I.   Title
328.41'073   JN677
ISBN 0–571–13627–3

Library of Congress Cataloging in Publication Data
Pearce, Edward.
Hummingbirds and hyenas.

1. Great Britain–Politics and government–1979–
I. Title.
DA589.7.P43 1985   941.085   85-10340
ISBN 0–571–13627–3 (pbk.)

'To My Friends Pictured Within'

Contents

Preface

This was conceived as a natural successor to *The Senate of Lilliput*. I was not best pleased when that work was catalogued by the British Museum as 'Facetiae'. *Hummingbirds and Hyenas* is certainly intended to amuse and to treat Parliament satirically, but I have also sought to assay the characters and quality of Parliamentary personalities. Nothing here is reprinted or cannibalized from journalistic work. It is a sustained essay on the characters of the House and its ways, stuck full of prejudice but informed by the long hours in the Press Gallery of a Parliamentary sketch-writer. His job is to be a Political Critic. *Hummingbirds and Hyenas*, despite the jokes, is intended as just that, Political Criticism.

E.P.

Acknowledgements

I should like to thank Miss Sally Hallam, Mrs Rita Walsh and my wife Deanna, who, in ascending order of work undertaken, helped produce a typescript fit for a publisher to see, and my wife (again) for the vast troubles taken with an exacting index of a book littered with names. Also, I wish to thank Frances Coady for her enlightened and inspiriting help as editor. Behind every book, good or otherwise, there appear to be any number of good women.

I

Into the Undergrowth

The shadows have been almost completely replaced.

'Politics is not about personalities.' Mr Heath said it; Mr Benn proclaims it – while denouncing the trivialization of politics. If we followed these stern improving attitudes, public interest in politics would be as extensive as public interest in structuralism! Politics is very solemn about itself but retains its attraction precisely because personality and trivialization make it tolerable.

The Senate of Lilliput, written in the latter part of 1982, was an attempt by an improvising, impressionistic and grossly biased hand to show the character and opinions, foibles and charms of the legislative class. It was a Who's Who (and frequently a Who's Nobody) of the Westminster *Nibelungs* with a special section on Mrs Wotan. Time has now passed. Mr Michael Foot is with God on the back benches; Mr Parkinson, taken in adultery, has been stoned to death; Willie Whitelaw has become a real Lord; at the Sepulchre in Smith Square Selwyn Gummer rules, not at all OK; the Labour Front Bench has been reshuffled like a new hand of strip poker and Mr Kinnock sits in his underpants.

Politics is absolutely about personalities. We have a whole new set of them. Or more precisely, politics has hired and fired, promoted, reshuffled, ennobled or sent away as Shadow Secretary of State for Scotland those who were with us in May 1983. The House has admittedly a large new intake, predominantly but not exclusively Conservative. Government with every

13

excuse for feeling pleased, was modestly amended; the Opposition Front Bench is under new management at almost every level with hardly a survivor doing the job he did before. The Straws, Cooks and Cunninghams, the Dewars and Prescotts have been swept, if not to power, then to its melancholy parody. The Shadows have been almost completely replaced.

The present House of Commons is the product of Mrs Margaret Thatcher's extraordinary success – in the narrowly political sense. It is lopsided with Tory good fortune. There are 394 of them to the 206 who obey, if they feel like it, the instructions of Labour's Chief Whip, Michael Cocks. Seventeen Liberals and six Social Democrats with a variety of Celtic oddments make up the residue. Whatever anyone says about Mrs Thatcher, and I am inclined to say quite a bit, she had an arithmetical political success on her hands, so large as to be embarrassing. The General Election which produced these results left Labour in a state of trauma. The Party had not been so low in the water since 1931. But the actual measure of Labour's defeat was actually worse, even though it held more seats. The standard comparison is with 1918, the Coupon Election held at a time when Labour was not a fully formed party contesting every seat. As I hope to show, Labour in the Commons, despite much better polls, has long sunk into demoralized mechanical devotions. The new leadership is not by any means a disaster, but to lead the Labour Party at that moment required the qualities of Washington at Valley Forge, or Alfred at Athelny.

After 1931 Labour could comfort itself with the knowledge that its numbers were grossly under-represented by seats. The Election itself, when Phillip Snowden had wandered around waving billion-mark notes as a warning of what might happen if tiny benefits were not cut yet further, was a fraud, indeed the very best sort of fraud, sincerely believed in by its perpetrators. Further, it was an operation garlanded by the defecting Leadership of Labour. Conservatives, not for the first or last time, were calling themselves by an alias. 'Vote National,' said Mr Baldwin and Mr MacDonald, Labour's respected Leader of the day before.

The defecting Labour Right of 1931 was getting things wrong, but that Election, dreadful as it was, represented a vicious jolt on an otherwise steady chart. Labour's arithmetic from the end of the First World War until 1955 was, with this aberration excepted, to grow single-mindedly better. In 1951 only a fit of foolish high-mindedness over the redistribution of seats, something in which Jim Callaghan would not have indulged, caused Labour, chivalrous and exhausted, with its biggest popular vote ever, to lose a majority in Parliament.

By contrast, Labour on the morning of 10 June 1983 knew that 206 seats were the least of its problems. The percentage poll not only showed a down drift dangerously close to the third party, but it was a secular drift. Labour has been losing votes for a long time now and not winning them back. In the South of England, apart from London, Labour held Ipswich and Bristol East; it was running third in constituencies and had lost a total of 119 deposits. All this did not come as a result of any nailable fraud. The redrawing of constituency boundaries had been absurdly overdue; the Falkland Islands dispute might indeed have been a wasteful irrelevance, but Labour (having seen the polls) had not had the nerve to say so. Above all, hard times, exactly like shortages under Mr Attlee, whose *popular* vote increased in 1950, had not injured the Government. And of course terrible results came after a decade of terrible quarrelling.

Labour Conferences had been conducted in the style of sixteenth-century Mantua. That Renaissance word, the *camarilla*, was at work everywhere. What the darker Italian Courts had called the *camarilla* Harold Wilson was to call 'a tightly-knit group of politically motivated men'. The long-fought-out campaign to transfer political power to the constituencies and to Conference, to reselect and choose the leader, had been won. The indirect effect of such demotion can be seen in the House of Commons, where Labour attendance in the Chamber has so declined that it resembles a stage army and a thunder-sheet. Labour attendance at prime parts of the day can be as few as six.

Look over the Gallery balcony and you will see them – a spokesman, perhaps in this case that least of aspiring things, a junior shadow, together with a whip, a specialist, two lugs from below the gangway and a man loitering at the bar before going on somewhere more interesting.

Where the rest are who knows. Not everyone is serving on the Police and Criminal Evidence Committee which preoccupied

1983–4. A few, no doubt, are with the Transport Committee in Vienna, Amsterdam or Tokyo, to name only three of the destinations of that golden and with-ticket skive. They cannot all be on a select Committee usefully asking the Chancellor and Mr Terry Burns thoughtful and constructive questions about the projected growth of M zero. For that matter they can't all be with their mistresses. Indeed since the truly sad case of Mr Gerald Bermingham, universally regarded as one of the bright, hard-working, intelligent people in the Labour intake and a notable force on that Police Bill Committee, but given to sleeping with more girls than his godly local executive had authorized, one suspects that a distressingly small number of Labour politicians will be so innocently occupied. Local committees of public safety increasingly take a view of illicit congress a couple of paces on the unforgiving side of Mary Whitehouse.

Some MPs are in their constituencies oiling up the people most likely to push them down the chute; a great number are dutifully employed in the Norman Shaw Building, a place where politicians go to feel like junior executives at IBM, dictating letters in decent seclusion. The club aspect of the House and the centre for pondered contributions attentively listened to are, like Nineveh and Tyre, not what they were.

Labour's low attendance went so far one dark night in May that it got down to nobody at all. Now substantial numbers should not be expected on an all-nighter. This phenomenon is an agreeable British eccentricity by which oppositions register their wholly furious antipathy to a piece of Government busi-ness by keeping everybody up till the milkman, doing no good but proving their seriousness. This indeed is an extension of the House's old club-like status, with the difference that the Commons becomes 'a little place that we could go on to'. Champagne is indeed possible in this rambling set of licensed premises, but for the most part tea is kept flowing for those on watch, while it is understood through usual channels that the generality will be trying to get some sleep on the premises, whips permitting. To this end Jim Prior was to be seen taking out of his car boot a large *Tugend* or continental quilt, quite the most useful contribution any member could make to a crisis.

On this occasion Labour was protesting the night away against Mrs Thatcher's democratic decision to make preparation to have the Greater London Council go the way of the Chilean parliament (as Labour sees things) and for Mr Kenneth Livingstone to be hung in irons from London Bridge. It was to have been the watershed of Mr Livingstone's brilliant campaign. For the Official Opposition to have responded with a row of zeds indicating deep and soothing sleep was an anti-climax so desolating as to indicate constructive resignation as an opposition. Sleeping sentries have, after all, commonly been shot.

Like Lord Lucky's assent to a dukedom, it happened in the following way: Labour had manned the ramparts sporadically but thinly through Wednesday morning but by about 6 am was down to its very last man, who not only slipped out but stayed slipped out, vacating the Opposition front bench and leaving the chamber naked of Labour members. Simon Hughes, the Liberal from Bermondsey, who has in all conscience done Labour quite enough harm already, took his place on the front bench beside the despatch box, the first Liberal to do so since 1924, and proceeded to talk out of his ear.

It was not important what Mr Hughes actually did say at that hour providing he kept on saying it. And, Welsh-descended as he is, he put up a fine frothing performance. But it took more than half an hour for the first Labour member to discover him. By the time the Labour whips had found out, John Biffen's friends had found out as well. Mr Hughes had motor-mouthed on for some time, and he had successors. Meanwhile Biffen's runners were rousing Tories from Commons offices and neighbouring homes to come and, as it were, talk in a totally new ball game.

Hitherto it had been in the Tory interest to shut up and indeed encourage rest among their members. Incidentally, if the previous Tuesday runs on till 2.30 am on Wednesday, Wednesday never happened: it is a sort of *chrissum* unbaptized, innocent of all sin and sent straight to Heaven. And if Wednesday was scrapped, the painful conclusions of the paving bill to facilitate the abolition of Ken and his chaps could, in the Commons, be pushed in (and through) here and now. It was not necessary to wait for the scheduled time when various Conservative Outs, Mr Rippon, Mr Pym and the discontented organist, would rise to embarrass everybody with their devotion to local government.

The short message conveyed by Mr Biffen through the whips was that now was the time for all good men to witter on in the aid of the Party. The fury on the Labour benches was not at all with this good generalship, a little with the Alliance for starting the mischief, but supremely with their own stumbling selves. As the hour of 2.30 approached two Labour men actually had to be restrained from coming to blows. As Teddy Taylor cruelly remarked, 'Labour are in no position to go on. They've had far too much sleep.' For Wednesday was to have been the date of the Official Opposition motion protesting at the long-overdue closure of the long-bankrupt Bathgate works, something which was restored to them only by governmental grace and favour, for another day.

The display of incompetence, negligence and sleepy indifference in respect of matters where the Party professed itself to be passionately committed lucidly illustrates Labour's general condition. It arises partly from the anti-parliamentary cast of mind of some of the Heavy Left in the new intake, but more powerfully from the want of conviction and will to win among the harassed generality. Obliged to speak in language more extravagant than their feelings, compelled to make every utterance with a quick glance over the shoulder at constituencies that delight in their probationary powers, Labour politicians have become ticket-of-leave men. They react variably to the outside pressure, some in a spirit of submissive but slowed-up loyalty, some angrily and with a disaffected contempt which spills outside while one eye contemplates other, less humiliating careers.

Demoralization stems from something else. The prospect of a Labour government is not very great, even to those Labour Members who still want a Labour government. At worst they felt terribly like the Cambridge boat. The Government's simple majority over the official Opposition alone is 190, only 16 fewer than Labour's actual total. It created the impression not of being dead, but of having been too long buried and ensepulchred under four tons of Portland stone. In such circumstances apathy, absence, preoccupation and want of a reasoned case will prevail even with improved polls.

It was all summed up very aptly by the Leader and Deputy Leader in their respective replies to the Budget in 1984. Kin-

18

nock's was supposed to be a brief back-of-the-envelope affair, since no one expects any leader of the opposition, sight unseen, to take on the heavy-metal back-up of a chancellor delivering a Budget. The considered reply comes at length next day from the shadow chancellor. From Neil we wanted eight minutes with three or four salient points sketched swiftly in. From Hattersley next day, with time to compose his thoughts, we expected a minumum of forty minutes of close analysis. Kinnock being verbose and Hattersley apathetic, we received respectively twenty-four and twenty-six minutes. 1985 was no better.

A consequence of official Labour's low attendance and perfunctory performance is that the Hooligans loom larger. Here one has a problem of definition. There are, as it were, accredited Hooligans sitting by sanctified tradition below the gangway. Mr Skinner and Mr Canavan are, by convention if not yet by statute, extensions of the Constitution. A newer element comprises Mr Roland Boyes, a man of cast-iron intellect; the Militantly Tending David Nellist who distinguished himself during Long Tuesday by asking a point of order at ten-past two and being nearly assaulted by colleagues, and the peculiarly foul-mouthed Tony Banks, who at the GLC is in charge of culture. One does not repeat the things Mr Banks says; God-fearing printers – for that matter electronic typesetting processes with a touch of discernment – would decline to set them on the page. The new horrors, aided by Screaming Ron Brown of Leith, that atom of public melancholy, play a disproportionate part. At the very least they are more noticeable. If we have more silly men in a smaller party whose sensible men are in a state of bruised and subdued anxiety, the importance of fools will expand.

Problems are thus created for the Speaker. Mr Bernard Weatherill is a different kind of man from his predecessor, George Thomas. He is not so incisive in dealing with trouble and, not having been brought up in the Labour Party, does not hate the left-wing rioters with the same low-burning, total contempt as his predecessor. George Thomas, made into a viscount in Mrs Thatcher's drive to restore the social pyramid, was the sort of Speaker government whips like. 'The Prime Minister has a right to be heard' was his recurring maxim. He was indulgent towards the front benches and inclined to use

19

martial law up-country. Long confinement in the Labour Party does funny things to people. It was a strong Speakership but not untouched by deference.

Mr Weatherill is quite the other way. A rather gentle character behind a gruffness he keeps working at, he has the fault of not quite letting his yea be yea and his nay be nay. If the Speaker draws a line then he should let nobody go across it. The only defect of Mr Weatherill is an occasional tendency to say, 'I will take no further interventions' and, after noises off, wearily to add, 'Oh, very well then.' But if he kicks this habit Mr Weatherill will be the better Speaker.

George Thomas tolerated the setting of dummy questions from creaturely Tory hacks about the conduct of the Leader of the Opposition. Mr Weatherill has abolished such free kicks with the curt reminder that the Prime Minister answers only for her responsibilities. He has also taken a much more liberal line on Private Notice Questions (PNQs), which, being detailed and slightly inquisitorial, are frequently unwelcome to government.

Mr Weatherill, apart from a stint as deputy chief whip, is essentially a backbencher's man. And the Opposition, if it had the spirit, could utilize the presence of a Speaker disinclined to get governments off hooks. It would do so by being detailed and difficult rather than silly. Even Question Time could be rescued from its present domination by ego-flapping publicists. Well-marshalled opposition with relays of serious, polite, difficult questions – something admittedly hard to imagine in the Labour Party's present condition – could put Mrs Thatcher under pressure. She is not going to be rescued by the Speaker, but at present she is protected by the Opposition. Mr Kinnock has reduced his word mileage and is sharpening up his act. But the intelligent exploitation of that very public fifteen minutes with relays of prepared questions from the grown-ups is not taking place and an opportunity is being lost.

The millstone grows heavier. A signal part of Labour's parliamentary membership is made up of people whom Sara Barker, the late magnificent National Agent in the days when Labour won Elections, would have proscribed.

The underlying reasons for the Speaker's approach is simple. He does not like Mrs Thatcher and she does not like him. To put it very plainly, she passed him over in 1979 for chief whip and did everything in her power to have him passed over for the Speakership in 1983. Politics buzzed for over a year about George Thomas's successor. The interesting names of Mark Carlisle, lately Minister of Education, Terence Higgins, a badly neglected parliamentary intelligence, and Norman St John-Stevas, growing morose but not wise out of his elemental limelight, had all been mentioned. Mrs Thatcher herself favoured Humphrey Atkins, a former chief whip reluctantly retired from the Foreign Office when it dropped the Falkland Islands into the sink. Such a man would be heavily obliged to her and being handsome of aspect would have adorned the Speaker's chair as a profile. It was extraordinarily foolish and improper in her to contemplate any such move.

We do not have a written constitution, as every schoolboy once knew; but we have understandings. And one of those understandings is that the Speakership is in the gift of the House of Commons. In practice this has often meant that it was in the gift of the 'usual channels.' Notoriously the Tory whips once offered the Labour whips a short list of Selwyn Lloyd and John Boyd-Carpenter, the Labour whips said, 'We prefer Selwyn' and thus was the will of the Commons expressed. Even by such standards, however, Mrs Thatcher's handling of the chair was unimaginably crude and queenly. It was reminiscent of the story told about Mrs Thatcher's rather grand behaviour as she waved to crowds shortly after her election in 1979, and the alleged murmur from the Palace, 'Tell the Prime Minister to do her job and we will do ours.' Such a base canard must be a tissue of lies and a gross libel on our client as Lord Goodman would say in one of his intimidating letters. But it catches the flavour of Mrs Thatcher on a high – the hauteur, the lack of sensibility and the assumption that one victory predicates universal submission.

This, rather than anti-democratic feeling, accounts for the banana skins which the British public from June 1983 onwards came to know as old friends. Mrs Thatcher is the best thing we have had in government since the days of Attlee and Bevin, but success definitely spoils her. It begets not authoritarianism but peremptoriness.

Mrs Thatcher made the first mistake of her first term's many mistakes. Mr Weatherill, who will do well to make life baron, runs the House in a style more liberal, less convenient, extra

PNQs and all, than she had intended. He might be wise however to tighten some screws. That finished primitive, Mr Dennis Skinner, has been permitted rights of free-range mithering such that a barbarous maunder runs through the attempts to speak of anyone standing remotely near him. And it took the authority of the Deputy Speaker, Harold Walker, an ex-miner ,with the patience of Cromwell, to throw the public menace out. Jack Weatherill is from some angles too kind. But in this over-manned, nervous and frustrated House, kindness is not altogether out of place.

Labour is unhappy because it is the party of 13 million votes gradually transformed into the party of 8 million votes. The Tories are unhappy because there are too many of them for distinction to be won or utility to be registered. The new backbenchers remind me a little in their frustration of the eldest son of Thomas Hardy's Jude. The little lad, so solemn in his ways, Gummer before his hour, was nicknamed 'Old Father Time'. And at a hard moment in the family's fortunes organized his brothers in a collective suicide – they hanged themselves in a cupboard – leaving behind the message, apt for the present Parliamentary Conservative Party – 'Because we was too many'.

As for the Alliance, they, with a high ratio of speeches to Members, are happy in the individual ego however embittered collectively at the absence of the proportional representation that has done such wonders for stable government in, say, Italy. The Alliance, with its twenty-three members – twenty-four since Patrick Jenkin told the electors of Portsmouth South that the city might be rate-capped – are the least unhappy. They are also watching with astonishment the phenomenon of their Leader – there is no other word for him – Dr David Owen. Officially the Alliance is a loose association of two parties, each with its individual head. In the last Parliament the Alliance with forty members was notable for non-percussion, for playing Wagner in palm court style, for having no effect at all. All is changed, changed utterly; or, as a greater mind would put it, the trivialization and personalization of politics has intruded. There is no getting away from personalities when you can find them. The transformation of David Owen from the prim mortician one remembers as Jim Callaghan's Foreign Secretary into a tempered and restrained ball of fire is quietly marvelled at. He has a voice which carries without tiresome shouting; having won authority he is wisely polite; he does not grow bored with a good point and hurry off frivolously pursuing a variety of bad ones. Repetition is good for you; in the right hands it can do for a politician what it has done for bottled stout. So the world knows that the Alliance, while supporting nuclear defence and despising CND, is against Trident on grounds of cost and general excess, and it thinks that writs and injunctions should have been issued against Arthur Scargill and his street troops.

These being such excellent points, iteration of them can only cut a profile of policy which no amount of rabbiting dialogue, no stupefying position papers could conjure up. The strength of Owen is that to a certain personal force he adds preoccupation with macro-politics. Two or three big issues sharply defined, no waffle, no on-going shredded wheat of tedious detail; by such means does a party out of office tell people what it is about. If the Liberals and their Conference did not exist, Owen could do wonders.

The meeting of a natural leader and a group that has found its own soft-spoken and conciliatory chief hardly bearable will induce hatreds of a kind long familiar to anyone with a passing acquaintance with the Labour Party. Owen is pitching, by instinct and judgement, to the Right, acknowledging the premises of the dry Tories, regretting their habit of pulling ugly faces as a prelude to pulling their punches. Between him and a party of cloudly leftishness, which doesn't understand life outside Liberalism, a party competent in the field and incompetent in the head, there is fixed not an abyss so much as a galactic leap. The near-exhaustion of David Steel, for all his ambition, common sense and Wilsonian relationship with his party, is clear enough evidence of the real nature of the Alliance. Owen is not fighting Steel, he is fighting Steel's battles.

People representative of that dreadful conference, the Liberal Assembly, are creeping into the dove-grey ranks of Parliamentary Liberals: the likeable Mr Ashdown whose views on Defence are all that Mrs Thatcher could ask of an opponent, and the not particularly likeable Mr Meadowcroft who seems to have assembled all the bigotries and resentments one medium-sized soul can properly accommodate. Like Michael Foot before

23

him, Mr Meadowcroft so loathes America that he has kept himself pure by refusing ever to go there.

If the position of the Alliance is interesting and full of prospective bumps and aspirations, that of the government party, its excessive numbers apart, is very odd. They are a moody, supersensitive lot, the Tories, up and down beyond reason. They are filled beyond the Left's understanding with self-doubt, much of it hideously well founded. If a couple of things go right, they send off for champagne, the silliest and most overrated form alcohol can take, a very Tory drink; a spot of the militant workers demanding their rights, while the Chancellor declares that the Economy is fundamentally sound, and they behave privately as Vienna opera-goers behave publicly. That party has all the built-in stability of the Hang Seng Index.

Since there have been a number of small cataclysms – one ticks off GCHQ, the Libyan Embassy, the GLC legislation, the pit strike, sterling, and the opinion polls – anxiety is perhaps reasonable. Even so it was very odd, thirteen months after June 1983, to hear a non-wet Tory say of a vote against the Government that while he would never join it or any other rebellion involving Mr Heath and Mr Pym, whom he despised, nevertheless she could not be permitted to lead the Party at the next Election. It was odder still to hear a Minister say of one prospective bad by-election result, 'Good' and of a potential worse one, 'Better.' I shall try later in this book to give an account of the rise, rise, wobble and who should say what next of Margaret Thatcher.

As it was, we were caught in the midsummer of 1984 with an odd mood of Westminster hysteria to which an undersized Alliance and a leaden, rote-reciting Labour contributed almost nothing. One disappointed backbencher, reduced in his business career to selling gilt-edged securities to West African politicians, gleefully pronounced the Prime Minister as good as assassinated. Strange stories circulated about some rural gathering called by Mr Francis Pym. According to Mr Pym, official sources were hysterically accusing him of playing Catesby to various friendly neighbourhood Fawkeses. It was implied that friends of Mr Pym had tried to set them up. As to who sets up whom in the devious world of press briefings and casual unimportant little gatherings I should not like to be the arbiter. But the corridors of Westminster that July in 1984 ran with hypothecated blood. At Oxford in 1985 he cut himself!

And yet, odd as it sounds, it is equally true to say that this new Parliament was, on the Tory side, initially less sectarian. There are convictions and strong beliefs yet the notion, so recurrent in 1980–1, that some sort of Jacobite counter-revolution could be effected, that a vast U-turn (inescapable cliché) could be described, perhaps under the wise guidance of Lord Carrington, is remote even as polls fall.

The broad economic policy of the Government, entrenched by Mr Lawson's Budget (the only thing that man should be let near) is still consensual. Sorrows may come in battalions, largely at the bidding of the American Supply-siders, those Keynesians in drag. How foolish that game has been with all its pleasures, how sensible, given our resources, the British, with all their pains! The rising interest rates of that summer were bad political news for the British Tories, but it was understood that they came from the overspill of somebody else's profligacy and that we must await the US deflation package.

The new intake of Tories, the subject of a later chapter, is not dreaming of reflation. They may be soft or hard in their social outlook, but the lesson of Mr James Callaghan that 'the day when we thought we could spend our way out of trouble has passed', which Mrs Thatcher has sewn into a sampler, has broad Conservative support. Trouble, when trouble comes, will be a matter of personnel. Has Mrs Thatcher overextended herself, grown unwise with too long a time in office, failed to keep backbenches sweet, worked too hard and too minutely, been oddly slow in her handling of Arthur Scargill whom many Conservatives wanted at once to see candidly fought, beaten and eradicated by clean little actions for exemplary damages? Has she lost the thread of things? Whatever pleasure Mr Pym may have taken at this time, one shrewd old practitioner observed, 'There may be Pymmery about but there are no takers for Pym.' If the Tories have a hero at the moment, apart that is from Dr David Owen, it is probably Eddie Shah, taker-on and beater insensible over a few days of the National Graphical Association, when they used tactics of violence distinguishable only in extent from the *Sturm Abteil* methods of the NUM.

These Members have a notion of losing when they should be winning, of government being paralysed by office, 'of letting "I dare not" wait upon "I would" like the poor cat i' the adage'. Indeed if things go *really* wrong for Mrs Thatcher she may yet be memorialized, not as an authoritarian, not as one whose approach was too resolute, but as a lady enmeshed in circumspection, as indeed, 'the poor cat i' the adage'.

Hummingbirds and Hyenas attempts to take on the movement of events: Mrs Thatcher in sustained trouble, the Official Opposition never quite having had an empire and attempting to persuade itself and the public that it has a role. Also we will concern ourselves with a larger sphere than *The Senate of Lilliput*, a book written with corroding affection entirely about the Chamber of the Commons. An attempt will be made to do justice, if that is what it deserves, to the House of Lords, a body which I candidly confess reminds me of nothing so much as a quango matched at stud with a memorial service. The Lords matters to some people, to Mr Ken Livingstone for one, to newspaper proprietors for another and to a certain sort of High Church, art-appreciating social trekker for whom eight balls on a coronet are better than six, but it is acquiring a certain constitutional utility. Since the House of Lords has been permitted, as the Conservative backbenches with their Malthusian problems have not, the sweet delights of chucking out substantive bits of Government legislation, it clearly counts. The Commons cannot tell Mr Tom King to be a touch braver and stick ballots into trade union legislation, nor can they haul Patrick Jenkin off the unwise substitution of a temporary committee for an elected council. The Lords, now delightedly on camera, can – but only to a Tory government. Under Labour they cringe in the shadow of the merciful hypodermic and would have voted through a bill to replace all elected bodies providing their own embalmer's prize entry was left intact. However, there they are, blessed with a little brief authority and we shall have to talk about them.

Finally, this side of getting oneself cut in the press canteen, it seems necessary to say something about the half-world of politics, the journalists who technically do not exist but who, like 'termites', in the over-excited phrase of Mr Andrew Faulds, move about upstairs in great numbers. Like two drunks, though

26

both professions are deplorably reformed from the incapable stupor of happier days, journalism and politics support each other; they find things to do, we find ways of describing them.

The function can be one of dutiful transmission of shorthand copy. It can be news gathered in by the lobby, which has to deal with what people, especially Government people, want it to think and what it can find out elsewhere. We are all of us, whatever our duties, like Dr Johnson's definition of a lexicographer, 'harmless drudges'. But we are also in-between people, something which makes us so like back-bench MPs that a special sympathy, in my view at least, exists between the two groups. We both look on; we both see a lot of the game; we can both grasp that the Secretary of State for Energy has got it wrong again, but the function which remains to us is to watch, warn and, if you chance your luck, deride.

That, come to think of it, aptly describes the broad objective of this book, as it attempts to hug the coast and rechart the recent cliff falls, erosions and eruptions, momentarily slipping off course to Bournemouth, Blackpool and the House of Lords, upon cold thankless seas of discovery.

2

Westminster-on-Sea

'We must capture the hearts of people, white or blue.' The tone is unmistakable. No practising politician has such a grasp of solecism. The appeal to workers without reference to race, creed or collar came from a floor speaker, Mr Charles Westerly, at a party conference. It could have been any party conference since they have an ecumenical tendency to pool their nonsense. But it chanced to occur during the Social Democrats' six-day voyage in 1982 from Cardiff to Great Yarmouth by way of Derby.

These travels, we protest in the newspapers, are dreadful. (The metropolitan condescension of journalists cast among fish-and-chip shops is a wonderful thing. But in fact we don't find any of these places dreadful; and the SDP by plunging into vertical and horizontal journeys (Cardiff – Derby – Great Yarmouth was preceded by Perth – Bradford – London) did make political life a degree more interesting.

The small parties are blessed, not that they would see it like that, with small conferences. The cruel logistics of numbers confines the Tories and Labour to a dull shuttle between the two towns that have the facilities – dull Blackpool and shiny Brighton. The Liberals can get their dinky outfit into somewhere nicer than either, like Harrogate or Scarborough or even Llandudno, that Edwardian film set, whose wrought iron and high-glazed brickwork belong with the last Liberal Government of Mr Asquith which faded into oblivion by way of coalition in December 1916. Though there are moments of despair when it might seem apt for the Liberals to book a week in late September at the Hippodrome, Nineveh.

Conferences are different to ordinary politics. They represent not just silliness and excess but also the essential characteristics of each party. Politicians at Westminster are sensibly corrupted by other politicians with whom they have to share their rambling palace,corrupted from the noisy, fierce partisanship of the junior activist into the unimpressable good humour of the working cynic. All conferences are betrayed. Labour ones yearn to abolish defence; a majority of Tory delegates would have liked to sustain the status quo in Rhodesia. Conference exists to celebrate the essences of politics precisely as Parliament and day-to-day administration exist to minimize them.

Labour made itself an exception to this rule by letting collegiate electoral power be taken up by the trade unions and by Conference itself. The people who worked hard and long to make the constitutional change knew what they were about. They distrusted large parts even of the Left in the Parliamentary Party. When Mr Benn made his pitch for the deputy leadership, he lost under the new rules by only 0.6 per cent. And, of course, a great tract of what would conventionally be called the Parliamentary Left, led by Stanley Orme and Neil Kinnock, voted for his defeat either directly or by giving support to the wrecking candidacy of Mr John Silkin. Thus was the Soft Left identified and, while we are about it, Mr Kinnock's own skilful and fortunate ascent to the leadership begun.

Labour Conference has by crafty irridentism made itself into a different class of conference from all the others. The Tories are amused at this Trusting of the People (for the very good reason that the people trusted are not the People, but a delegate congress, something very different). The Liberals, by contrast, have a genuine yearning for open-hearted, open-headed public forum democracy – they don't call their conference an assembly for nothing. But in actual oily-rag and adjustable-spanner terms they have a constitution remarkable for its illiberalism. The Liberal Assembly is in favour of unilateral nuclear disarmament. Mr Steel, who is in favour of having a lot of MPs, is not. Accordingly Mr Steel takes note of the Liberal Assembly's views. If you are one of the Liberal activists, Mr Tony Greaves, say, or Mr Michael Meadowcroft, able to produce radical majorities but with almost no perceptible effect, the yearning for a version of Labour's Periclean system, geared to the wishes of sedulous attenders of meetings, is considerable. There is going to be a small war inside that party and anyone who looks at the long-term prospects of the Liberal–SDP Alliance has to include in his calculations the effect of such a conflict in which very few prisoners will be taken.

One is tempted into faint sympathy with rebels. Political parties are seen very widely as the instruments of wise governors who appear, Soviet-style, for group photocalls and who, through representatives, make their wishes known. A rough time never did any politician any harm but nothing more readily reconciles the onlooker with the men at the top of a party than the views and style of those throwing things at them. The cry of 'Let's be with Sinn Fein' from a young thing at the Labour tribune says a good deal for the instincts of the Tories never wholly to abandon Lord Liverpool's view of the gross public. To quote casually phrases as casually noted down: 'The insane witch-hunt launched by the right-wing of the party'; 'The frenzied raving lunatic herself' (Mrs Thatcher); 'Rioting is not the answer, suicide is not the answer, nor are alcohol and drugs; the answer is the Labour Party Young Socialists' and 'If this movement doesn't transform mankind by the end of the decade, it will not be a case of Hiroshima, it will be the end of mankind.' These utterances all came at Labour Party Conference and thus represent the views of delegates who, in terms of the leadership election, have a percentage of finger on the trigger.

Neither the Liberal nor the SDP conferences are so bloodshot in their discourse, though whether we have to take seriously a delegate to the SDP Conference who advised us to resist the Soviet Union in the manner of Gandhi is a matter of judgement. The broad awfulness of Labour Party Conference, always the most genuinely open, despite the block votes, and which across the years became steadily more intolerant, more malevolent until thirty of its MPs actually left, stands as instruction to the other parties.

Fun can be had at the expense of the Tories, intended like ants to obey their genetic programming. The Tories fully appreciate that they run the most boring of all the conferences. Rebellion does occur, as in 1981, but a Tory rebellion has to be followed, like a change of policy in *Pravda*, by way of code words and polite formulae. 'Disraeli', 'compassion' and 'One Nation' limp to mind. Labour are of course more candid and truthful as they wish one another into the Hell intended for the cream of the damned, but they do not thus advance their case with the public.

There are psychological differences between the parties as interesting as any contained in policy. Somebody once remarked that soccer was a game for gentlemen played by hooligans, while rugby was a game for hooligans played by gentlemen. Similarly Conservative Conference has individualism proclaimed by conformists, while at Labour's forum conformism is urgently demanded by ungovernable and fiercely competing private souls. Though one must not stress too hard the conventional nature of Tory contributors. Inside every Tim the accountant who comes to the tribune there is Rodney, the secondary banker, trying to get out. But there is, God knows, a dreadful amount of promiscuous servility at the Tory gathering. Chairmen are all forwarded from that sinister and mysterious organization, as little fathomed as the Tongs of China – the National Union. They function as the NCOs of the Conservative Party, expecting (and getting) obedience. Though their urgent loyalty occasionally yields delicious lapses as with the chairman who said, 'I can't take any more speakers now. I want to call Sir Geoffrey Howe.' Unlike Labour chairmen who are members of the National Executive and thus include a smattering of parliamentary and trade union great folk, Tory chairmen come from below stairs in the hierarchy. They can and do terminate a speech on the grounds of its being too strong or critical and they act with dismaying unction in proclaiming the grandeur of some Cabinet spokesman, listing his glories and calling for rapturous treatment: 'Now, ladies and gentlemen, I know you will want to give Mr Plantagenet-Bloggs who has come all the way from the Department of the Environment to speak to us, a response which shows how much we appreciate the wonderful work he has been doing.' It is hideously like *Listen with Mother*: 'Are you sitting comfortably? In a moment Michael Heseltine will be with you.'

Actually it is pretty nauseating. The Tories are not stupid. Socially they are changing beyond recognition. (In the words of one of my older Conservative friends, 'There are now a great number of lower middle-class people present.') Yet this still goes on. Some sort of adjustment from this dismal nurse-telling-infant-to-stand-up-and-kiss-Uncle-George-who-as-a-special-treat-is-going-to-show-them-his-slides simply has to be made.

The present system brings out the worst in delegates; and among seaside Conservatives there is a lot of worst to be brought out. They become incoherent with devotion to the party line. I shall not lightly forget Miss Eve Falkner supporting the EEC and putting the Americans in their proper colonial place: 'We have plugged in our umbilical cord across the Channel; it will not stretch across the Atlantic'; nor does one any more readily forget Mr Christopher Prout, also addicted to the vision of Strasburg, who proclaimed that 'without the EEC we should be a fourth-rate Albanian siege economy'. Then there was the heavy-breathing fan who wished that 'Lord Soames could come back to the tribune and deliver again the marvellous speech he made earlier.'

One gets a preview of horrors yet to be seen in Westminster when the snapping and combative young parliamentary candidate comes on flow. A painful memory is of Mr Jerry Hayes (the Tories being heavily into demotic diminutives) to whom I took in October 1980 a deep and prescient dislike. I quote from the Master: 'One had the ominous sinking feeling that, with his mini-cab driver's felicity, Mr Hayes has the makings of parliamentary selection about him.' He had!

The worst is not brought out only in humble seekers after winnable constituencies. Mr Prior, knowing that the specific will cause displeasure, used to hold a small festival of generality, broadly in favour of goodness and generosity being better than badness and malice, which would leave the notion of goodwill towards all men looking narrow and logarithmic.

Happily conference is also a time for all bad men to come to the aid of the party and to stage, behind the forms of Bourbon civility, a contest for the hearts and minds of the peasants. This, as any peasant knows, is best won by dropping napalm on them. No other description adequately takes in the prospect of Mr Heseltine and Mr Tebbit snarling at one another as they shape up for the leadership contest of 1989. The world-famous 'on your bike' speech of 1981 (actually it was, 'My dad got on his bike and went to look for a job' but let's not be pedantic) had its roots in a speech by Heseltine, which implied that the condition of his beloved Liverpool could be put right only by lots of public money, a 'U-turn' in policy and more power for caring, sharing Michael.

Mr Heseltine pitched at that precarious time, as he would not so emphatically pitch today, for the compassionate and scared votes; Mr Tebbit for the cheerful deflators and the lynchers of local-government officials. Ironically, in real life back at Whitehall, the execution of tough policies does not fall to a seaside orator but becomes the responsibility of one of those civil servantly politicians: Mr Patrick Jenkin, for example, exists to carry out under fire nationally what has been proclaimed to rapture among party activists. Politics has a brutal way of dividing between Sherpas and Mountaineers. The Sherpa carries everything with exactly as good a chance of falling down a fissure as his master. The Mountaineer is content to show the way. The Sherpa goes everywhere except to the top while the Mountaineer has a mountain named after him, gets on television and writes his memoirs. The speeches of Sherpas at party conferences may be significant, but they are not recalled. Conference for them is an interlude before returning to the baggage train and the evasion of abominable snowmen from the Greater London Council come to disrupt it. The working rule is that whatever turns them on at Brighton will turn them out in the mass lobbies. Conference is thus pregnant with legislation and legislative disruption yet unborn.

In fairness, any Tory minister – Mountaineer or Sherpa – is assured of a soft ride. (Exceptional cases like the heckling of John Davies over Central African negotiations are precisely that – exceptional, a whiff of right-wing opinion couched in Labour Party terms.) They are no guide by which to navigate at all. A Soviet observer at Tory Conference remarked approvingly, 'This is how we organize *our* conferences.' And the affinities are extensive – too much hem-kissing, too little rebellion, the platform failing to be carried unanimously only on those ignominious occasions when it is carried overwhelmingly. For in truth the Conservatives, like the Germans, have learned democracy by numbers. It does not come naturally to them. It is not many years since the Leader (an unhappy title never used so baldly or so often by the other parties) stayed away from the vulgar forum until sweeping in, on the last day, after half an hour of warm-up and Wurlitzer, to the sort of un-British ecstasy we can do without. Now, out of deference to the age, they come to the daily sessions like the leaders of other parties; but on the last day – Friday afternoon or Saturday morning – they still do the Nuremberg bit. One jokes, but it is more than risible. The whole orchestrated thing with its five-minute minimum standing ovation, its blue drapes, amplified Elgar beforehand and pauses for the applause to come in like brass and woodwind, belongs in another age, another country and a different polity. The Court and Constitutional Party of Transcarpathia might properly behave like this. The English Tories, the last people on God's earth to trust the people, might experiment with growing up.

Not that one makes greater claims for Labour in the field of adulthood. The best alibi for the nursery tea of Conservative Conference is the rough company and bad habits respectively got into and picked up by the main Opposition. If one year Brighton is a sycophants' cake-walk then Blackpool will be unarmed combat (for those not carrying knives). Mr Derek Hatton made his début long before suspending the rules of local-government finance in Liverpool: he described Labour MPs who had left the Party as 'that treacherous rogues' gallery'.

But that is the merest ice-lolly compared to what you *can* hear. To quote a selection chosen at random: 'Bloodsuckers on the backs of the workers', 'parasites', and 'They stand in relation to Socialism like vampires to a crucifix.' Mr Peter Shore once remarked, 'Do not be so simplistic as to shout slogans.' In the election for leader – this writer's most grievous miscalculation – Mr Shore received 3 per cent of the college of MPs, trade unionists and Conference-goers. Another politician had said, 'Given the unremitting anger of working-class people and their kids, we must be the fist point of that anger' and had added, 'They cripple our children and taunt them for being lame.' Staying simplistic and shouting slogans, Mr Neil Kinnock got himself elected.

A Labour Conference is awful in a quite different way to the awfulness of a central committee meeting the week before at the other seaside town. There is comradeship and good nature. There are a lot of qualities appropriate to a party some of whose members were drawn to it for generous reasons. But the virtues are awash in the corrosive vituperative language of floor and platform. Some of this, to be scrupulous, is an old and innocent tradition. 'He is a traitor to the movement who should be hanged, chopped up and boiled in pitch' is Labour vernacular for 'I think old Fred is wrong about that one.' A measure of sulphurous excess is characteristic of working-class politics and amounts to no more than bladder-and-stick bravura, which other social classes, taking it at face value, comprehend with difficulty. But this will not explain away the amount of sheer hatred built up over the years as the parliamentary element, especially if they had been in government lately, were treated like public enemies in a Chinese court. In the really bad years there was a touch of the Cultural Revolution about. Denis Healey's crack about some of his colleagues being out of their tiny Chinese minds was not altogether a joke. There is an element, largely unacknowledged, of the sort of populism where the crowd is a weapon menacingly brandished in the faces of nominal, doomed leaders before they are broken and disgraced. It makes the Soviet-style nannying by the Tories of their adherents positively liberal by comparison.

Labour MPs usually sit on a special tier of seats, not as a privilege but for administrative convenience. In recent years they have looked like nothing so much as the French First Estate at the gathering of Louis XVI's unwise attempt at constitutional government.

Speak against the received norm with any force as some brave individuals do and expect to be shouted down. Go with unapproved ideas and make the sort of cowed and frightened speech that Mr Callaghan gave uncharacteristically in 1979, and you will be allowed the sufferance of derision. Go as the Ranting Left and you will produce results better not contemplated.

Some civility is owed to the Liberals and Social Democrats with all their faults. There can be a hundred sillinesses but the worst faults of the great parties are avoided. Dr Owen is masterful in a way that women's fiction and the Conservatives would understand. It must be the habit of saying 'scalpel' and being given a scalpel that has so habituated him to command. Plymouth Devonport, told to re-elect him, would not have had the nerve to do otherwise. But this useful tinge of the Great Khan apart, the Social Democrats, having got away from the Labour party without joining the Tories, are pretty keen to be as unlike both as possible.

A certain regard for American styles is apparent when they are in funds, usually expressed in political literature too glossy and well executed quite to fit with the flat ephemeral pamphlet favoured by most parties. They are also, never forget it, the party of Mrs Shirley Williams, no longer in Parliament but by reflex and profession the most reasonable, soft-spoken and temperate person in British politics. The Shirley style – quiet, conversational, never claiming the earth – is a major virtue, whatever mistakes Mrs Williams may have made as a Minister. 'Don't blackguard the other side. Let them do it to you and say how sad you are that they are letting themselves down.'

Mrs Williams long ago realized that the public detest the foam-rubber shillelaghs of partisan debate and would like to be treated with more respect. As a general rule that is the SDP and the Liberal way, though the Liberals play wonderfully dirty in by-elections and also have grave problems, which will get worse without the reward of success. It would be easy to remark that however civil their conduct and *douce* their address these people are out of power and doomed to hold only a handful of seats. Easy, wrong and premature. It is a vulgar error that serious people in the other parties will not be making.

But for the two smaller parties, conference is always a likely asset. The Tories perhaps expect some mileage out of their whipped hounds, but cannot expect to endear people by exposure of stage machinery, which, though dripping with oil, creaks. As for Labour, the vague feeling is that, as with accused persons hurried into court on serious charges, they might improve their chances by wearing blankets over their heads.

The Liberals, despite friction, and the SDP, despite inexperience, can count upon being better liked after a week's television. They are popular with the media notwithstanding the boringness that goes with decency, not least for their choice of venue, a merit very nearly erased from the face of the earth when the SDP, in a spirit of gay parody, chose in 1983 to visit Salford. But even the smaller parties have their moments of panic and disaster, like the SDP train which, travelling from Derby to Great Yarmouth, unaccountably stopped dead in the desert of rural Cambridgeshire producing the promise, carried through the corridors by a railwayman, that we should have a new train in March. Visions of living rough six months in the Fens ended only with the recollection that March, Cambridgeshire, is a town on the map. That stoppage or rather the long second delay at Norwich railway station which extended the fun, also had an outraged Roy Jenkins marching up and down the platform until, through a carriage window, he saw Dr Owen, not at that moment his favourite person, giving an *al fresco* press conference on mistakes in party leadership. The sealed train bearing Lenin and the carriage in the woodland clearing at Compiègne where Pétain signed the French surrender were joined in railway history by the train where Dr Owen's rise to the command of the entire Alliance was launched.

Because the SDP is inexpert, because it travels from centre to centre, because it has better quality officers than it has quantity of infantry, its leaders must speak early and speak often. They must do for themselves what Labour and Conservative politicians have done for them by aides, runners and hit men. They are vulnerable to more technical disasters: like the van carrying the stage scenery that breaks down on the East Anglian roads at the same time as that train carrying the press and the leaders is breaking down on the East Anglian railways. In consequence, half the secretariat is still up at 8 am tacking up cardboard logos in the Yarmouth Marina. It is all great fun. Little parties don't carry spares; big parties have somebody carry spares for them.

The serious error into which the SDP has slipped at its conference has been a desire to ram into the public gullet more programmes and policy than the public tummy will quite bear. Early taunted with having no policies and, in conjunction with the Liberals, leading the polls with 51 per cent of the vote, they produced policies like a pasta factory on overtime and (not entirely for this reason) finished with 22 per cent of the vote.

The Liberals have more acrimony and, despite Mr Steel's skills, are heading for the first negative and damaging conference yet if they are not careful. At conference the three parts of the Liberal Party come together like gunmen into a well-policed frontier town. The saloon smoulders with unconsummated shoot-outs, but the guns have been deposited with the sheriff earlier.

That party splits into three – Mr Steel's personal housecarls: Mr Moore, Mr Holme, the Parliamentary Party minus Cyril Smith and Councillor Meadowcroft – the Young Liberals: a bunch of gay liberationists, unilateral disarmers and getters-out of Northern Ireland now; and the ALC (Association of Liberal Councillors) who used to be *apparatchiks* good at getting out the vote and slicing the logistics but who have listened lately to the gospel of Councillor Meadowcroft and Mr Tony Greaves. These two are primitive anti-Americans and leftist populists with deep personal distaste for David Steel and conventional liberalism. Mr Steel's experience of conference is not markedly different to that of Harold Wilson and James Callaghan; he dreads it. It is an occasion for being applauded by the generality for the set-piece speech and nagged at, undermined and overruled by permutations of resentful town councillors and boy militants at whom the Labour Party would draw the line.

All student groups in all parties are an embarrassment. Labour tries to ban them; the Conservatives clench their teeth and say how splendid the young people are. The Liberals endure the deadly self-importance of the elderly young like Mr Peter Hain and Mr Simon Hebditch who call press conferences to announce their belief that Socialism can better be obtained outside the Liberal Party, which has betrayed them, and that accordingly as from 11 o'clock that morning they have defected. They do that if the Liberals are lucky; sometimes they insist on staying. They stay to campaign against Mr Steel before graduating like one Louis Eaks to work for better understanding with Colonel Gaddafi.

The Liberal Conference *is* an asset but a wasting one. The full suicidal rant of Labour in a bad year when votes are torn up and chucked in the fire with every successive loon who froths at the tribune will never be achieved. The old soft sell, based upon genuine good will, ginger beards, woolly pullovers and the broad style of a politically motivated coffee morning, still subsists. But the Liberal Leader, whose television manner keeps him fifteen statistically tested points clear of any other politician, cannot count upon the tolerance of his party indefinitely. Indeed Mr Steel's own highly publicized holiday from politics relates to rumbling moods within his party which are most apparent at conference time.

What has made life more dangerous is the alliance with the Social Democrats. The majority of Liberals vaguely approves of the notion, but those who dislike the SDP make up in the quality of their dislike for their minority status at large. And at conference they, like all evilly intended men, are over-represented. That is what party conferences are for, as Mr Scargill could explain.

The combination was voted in by a majority of sixteen to one when first mooted. Yet even on that promising day when God was in His Heaven and the post of prime minister designate was on offer, the response to Councillor Meadowcroft (agin the alliance) was impressive. Mr Meadowcroft now has a seat in Parliament, won in Leeds, to the lasting sorrow of Mr Steel's friends, by six votes in 1983. He is the voice of local Liberalism, narrow, petty, resentful of all non-Liberals, unsmooth, uncorrupted, untravelled and mindful that foreigners begin at Nottingham. He spoke against the alliance with characteristic courage when it was at its most popular. His large ovation suggested that what head approves heart cannot abide. After an electoral defeat for the combination, after two years of squabbling for precedence between two parties trying to put up one candidate at each of 500 or so constituencies, Mr Meadowcroft and his friends will have an easier time in the years ahead in their clear purpose to remove Mr Steel from the Liberal leadership. Any move against him would fail now, but the steady animus of his enemies is wearing him down. No obvious or commanding successor exists and the opportunities for the Liberals to do themselves immeasurable harm at conference this year, or one or two years on is very great. For the moment they smile nicely, and, when their Assembly comes on the screen, take credit for moderation and mutal tolerance.

There are some conferences that have nothing to lose in terms of image or good will. What they don't have they can't lose. Accordingly the anxiety of the Liberals, who balance a tray heavy with Meissen in a teashop unsuited to violence, are in a quite different case from the TUC, which, in terms of the metaphor, is sitting on the floor drinking tea out of pint mugs.

The TUC is less important to public politics now that Mrs Thatcher and Mr Tebbit have taken over industrial relations than at any time since Bonar Law. Conspicuously nobody is waiting for the TUC to be nice to them as a precondition for believing in the future. If the Employment Minister eats sandwiches and drinks tinned Worthington, he does so alone and for the depraved pleasure involved, not as an aid to negotiation at 3 am.

As a consequence of that, and of rather more important matters, TUC Conference has changed drastically for the better in recent years. Lately Mr Arthur Scargill has had three-quarters of the miners out on strike. He first held court in Sheffield, the Bayreuth of the cult, where an amenable delegate conference, encouraged by 2000 pickets around the building and the grievous bodily harm done earlier in the dispute, has voted to rig the rules.

But see Scargill at the seaside, away from his army with only a thin claque to bawl for him, and you understand the role of the crowd in anti-democratic politics. The contempt for Scargill of the TUC regulars is beautiful. In 1983 he spoke, if that is quite the verb I want, to an audience split between those who looked as if they were getting beer money to cheer and those whose lips curled in pleasurable embarrassment. Away from his mob, the man sounded like the Florence Foster Jenkins of debate. Miss Jenkins, it will be recalled, was a lady who, not being able to sing, paid people to listen and who made recordings while doing to the Queen of the Night's song things better left unmentioned.

Per contra Len Murray, who has spent many a miserable day trying to make noises that were expected of him, came into his own in 1983. There was a motion before Congress for a one-day strike. It was recommended, said Mr Murray, as a first step – 'Where to? Oblivion? There will be no blank cheques to break the law. This motion is not to be taken seriously. I haven't time to talk about it. Dismiss it.' That is not the unnerved and bullied subordinate of the past. The extent to which the Government's political victories and trade union legislation have given sensible men at the TUC freedom to *be* sensible should not be missed. Not that we lack clump-headed lugs keeping up ancient traditions. To hear Mr Ron Todd of the Transport Workers or Mr Alan Sapper of the £80,000-a-year TV cameramen's union is not to be enlightened.

Mr Todd argues for the peaceful intentions of the Soviet Union in the style of Bill Sykes, while Mr Sapper, who looks as if a kiss from the right girl might turn him into a prince, snarls for the working class, on behalf of a country club union whose typical member, at the expense of the TV licence, is on to his second Maserati.

But although the TUC has its full quota of people who could be exhibited for profit, there is less rabble-therapy than at some party conferences. Partly this is because the numbers are fewer, partly because the serious Hard Left, here exemplified by Mr Ken Gill of the British Communist Party, utter their menaces conversationally, partly because the unions are weaker and know it and finally because the death or incapacity of Mr Moss Evans has left a hole in the apparatus of the Far Left. The T. & G., which is to this great movement of ours what Trinity is to Cambridge scholarship or Christ Church to Oxford snobbery, grows ever more fissiparous. Mr Evans, weak, periodically very sick, afflicted with family misfortunes and not exactly Bismarck in the best of circumstances, had conceded that his control had diminished and he cannot always deliver the vote on promises made. For Lord Murray this state of affairs was the equivalent to being Holy Roman Emperor in a bad year for Prussia. The unions have been a good deal more sober in their utterance lately. They are into damage limitation, necessary and practical deals with Mr King, the painful work of assembling the shards left from the lost age of union supremacy – Jones-and-Scanlon, money on the table, social contract, legislation forwarded for approval and champagne settlements. TUC Conference has become instead a mixture of hangover and archaeology, with an increasingly sharp-tongued Professor Murray clutching his head with one hand while, with the other, he reassembles the remnants of a buried civilization.

Not surprisingly the serious men (who include the leaders of large unions not involved in the Labour Party for the good reason that their members have declined to affiliate) respond to the Scargill performance with the despair of adults in the presence of a hysterical adolescent. The loneliness of the bald and ginger figure shouting to his private group and despised by the baronage was very apparent. Unions, with all their faults, deal in realities. Their conference is capable of registering lost power and seeking new accommodations. The element of fantasy which lingers about the party shows, is more perfunctory here. The membership receipts have been counted and found wanting. The days of dispensing consent to Downing Street are a Babylonian recollection. Socialist revolution by the methods used at the Saltley coke depot is undesirable to many and unimaginable to most; while its principal advocate has all the affection among his unamused peers of a vexatious bagpiper in a built-up area.

Even in 1984 when immoderate men looked big and when Mr Scargill was to be received by the Labour Party at Blackpool like Her Majesty in the Solomon Isles, the TUC, though faced with special reinforcements of paramilitary pickets and making concessions under this threat that it ought not to have made, at least managed to look coerced rather than enraptured. Compare, as illustrations of this, the speech Neil Kinnock made on picket violence to the TUC with what he had to say within weeks to the Labour Party. At the TUC it was possible to be unequivocal; in front of the Labour delegates he tried to give the impression of being preoccupied with the sins of the police at the picket line while leaving little hints and clues about his distaste for the Kray Brothers aspect of certain Yorkshire pickets where a sharp eye for small print would find them. At the TUC Scargill received a partial standing ovation under pressure. At the Labour Conference he received two – at the start and at the end. In sexual terms, we witnessed the distinction between domestic acquiescence and nymphomania. (And if the TUC gets a chance it will put arsenic into his tea.)

The year of George Orwell provided fairly spooky conferences all round. The Liberals lurched nearer to a break with their Leader, with most of the Parliamentary Party and with the SDP on the subject of Defence. Also if they have not found an adequate replacement they have at least an aspirant in Mr 'Paddy' Ashdown, whose passion for intervening as the darling of the floor on every issue from world peace to ring roads earned him the title 'Mega-star' from a Young Liberal newssheet and a yearning for a pre-emptive number 11 bus from his parliamentary colleagues.

The Liberals, with Mr Ashdown at the head of the charge, have voted for a unilateralist position and have rejected the compromise nuclear freeze cunningly dreamt up by the Liberal Council. Indeed if one thing shines out of the Liberal Conference it is the gap – in principles and outlook – between the Council and the members. Liberal Assembly is a slightly random affair attended by those who want to go, and is not necessarily representative of the party back in the constituencies. What is for sure is that factions, the *camarillas* of politics, are avidly at work in that party. The Liberal Party is like a postcard cottage with roses over the lintel, ivy on the walls, hollyhocks in the front garden and matrimonial estrangement in the parlour.

A distinction exists between Labour and Liberal conferences, not least one of social class. But quite enough embarrassing things are said by Liberals, especially in 1984, not a happy conference year. 'The warmongers in the US and Britain,' said Mr Gavin Grant in the style of Mr Gromyko. He also attacked the 'rampant and virulent Republican party' but being a nice cosily muddled Liberal he called it the 'rampant and virulent *Democratic* Party'. Councillor Meadowcroft, now – at the expense of nice Joe Dean – a Member of Parliament, looked forward to the withering on the bough of NATO but regretted 'the Soviet knee-jerk reaction' that had brought on this deplorable Afghanistan business. But then naturally the Russians were worried about the provocative Cruise and Pershings 'so near to the motherland'. Mr Meadowcroft, whose droning voice reminds me of nothing so much as badly assembled air-conditioning, was seen at Bournemouth as a deep thinker. The author of several pamphlets and a very fair jazz clarinettist, he ranks here as Renaissance Man. Ranks, that is, in the eyes of the Young Liberals, an autonomous group who could be seen through glass doors caucusing in the Savoy Hotel at 1.15 am. They then throw up such charmers as Mr Pat O'Callaghan who on the question of the pit strike denounced the motion as 'a cheap exercise in NUM-bashing'. What anyway, he added, was all this rubbish about condemning the NUM for not holding a ballot? However, the difference between the two conferences is that although the Liberal platform has troubles with a very unpleasing youth movement belonging far to the left of it and suffers frequent reversals, that platform is still in charge and fighting back. It has in no way reached that condition of battered, broken-nerved, defeat-rationalizing marginality which is the last refuge of the Labour Right. The young Liberals, ardent mimeographers of the passing scene, rushed out a press release to coincide with the mines debate. The whole debate, they claimed, 'had been stage-managed as a media event . . . to condemn the strike and assure the leadership of a few good tabloid headlines'. Well, of course it had; and wouldn't Neil

Kinnock, sitting among the *bad* tabloid headlines, like to stage-manage something?

The Liberal platform, though frequently defeated, is still broadly in charge and the opposition groups headed by Mr Meadowcroft and Mr Ashdown are frustrated, despite the victories they win. The platform still dares to be unfair to them. When they complain about such unfairness, solid hunks of the national Establishment like Lord Tordoff are called in to say, 'Look, chaps, we've got this television thing pointing cameras at us and a row like this isn't doing us any good at all.' At which the non-rioting delegates burst into relieved and gratified applause and the Young Liberals mutter into their beards. You would make Lord Tordoff's speech at Labour Party Conference the way you would put your head on a railway line.

Also it is hard to imagine Labour receiving warmly the fraternal message of Mr Roy Jenkins, who rather sweetly called for us to keep up the 'spirit of Llandudno' and called for 'a bit of love between the two parties'. Middling Liberals, happy to keep up the spirit of Llandudno, constitute a solid majority of the national party. The Young Liberals rather bear out the saying in Proverbs: 'Iron sharpeneth iron; so a man sharpeneth the countenance of his friend', a good text for Mr Steel to contemplate. The Liberal platform, guided by the excellent Richard Holme, a party civil servant regularly burnt in effigy by the activists, has an altogether sharper countenance than the Labour platform. What it doesn't like it takes note of. It remembers very strongly the Liberal voter and potential Liberal voter and has before its eyes the example of the Labour Party whose leaders sit not so much on a platform as a scaffold.

They also look with a touch of envy at the SDP. At Buxton Mr Jenkins, who does very well away from the Labour Visigoths who surround him in the Commons, remarked, 'We get on with one another so well that we hardly qualify as a party at all!' It is fashionable to mock the Social Democrats. I have done some mocking myself, but after the party conferences of 1984 never again. They are a whit short on humour and their stage review was not awfully good, but after the other parties they are wonderfully civil and incidentally up-market. 'We are', said Mr Charles Brown of Newcastle, 'a liberal bourgeois society sympathetic to, but not much motivated by, notions of social justice.' Such rationality, such syntax! The SDP is also a leader's paradise. That is not just another observation about the happy condition of Dr Owen, of whom more in a moment. This is the one party, apart from the hem-kissing, *beni oui-oui Effendi* Tories, in which membership of Parliament is not a plague sore to be kept decently concealed. It must have the highest intelligence quotient among its rank and file of all four parties. (A friend of mine, formally a Labour MP, announced on his defection that he had attended his first SDP meeting: 'I think I was the only one there without a second degree.')

A certain seriousness, a whiff of academe and an inability to create headlines are the chief defects of the SDP Conference, mild failings compared to the others. There was also at Buxton in 1984 a sense of having put their act together. Nothing got lost on the road as happened in 1982 for the very satisfactory reason that the party didn't go on the road. Beautiful, if austerely hosteled, Buxton was a pleasant place to be in, and that element of amateurishness which characterized early conference is being dispelled. The quality has gone up no end.

There are advantages in being a small party. You can argue conversationally, you don't have to go to Blackpool, and a strong leader is able to speak with authority and be in receipt of affection. If Dr Owen was relaxed it was because he could afford to be relaxed. The Party may be modest but it is homogenous; it is far more serene than the Liberals are. (The real troubles start between the two halves of the Alliance.) In consequence Owen delivered a rather classy speech unfettered by the need to accommodate contradictions: 'I don't mind if my proposals are rejected. A leader should put up ideas and you should reject them if you think they are wrong.' One doesn't have to take Dr Owen comprehensively at his word. I rather think he likes being agreed with. But it is a happy notion and one which carries far more credibility at this conference than anywhere else in the circuit. It was not the way of Mr Heath, nor is it of Mrs Thatcher, to 'put up ideas and not mind them being rejected'. The Labour leader by contrast will hold whatever opinions he is given and will like them. Dr Owen spoke figuratively about throwing pebbles into the pool of ideas. Labour leaders don't throw, they duck.

If there has been an unhappier conference than Labour's at Blackpool last year I would prefer not to think about it. (There was, and those who were there when the bomb went off don't care to think about it either.) The memory of Miss Louise Christian describing the police as 'the salmonella poisoning in the sandwich', and of Mr Roy Maddox heralding the year 1939 and directly linking the present Government with the Nazis will not quickly go away. They were merely low points in a vituperating irrational rhetoric which dominated the Conference. The only piece of sustained good nature came from the Black delegates who rejected, or had rejected for them by conference, proposals for 'Black Sections', a notion more appropriate to Pretoria than Blackpool. A succession of Brown and Black speakers – a witty man from the Communications Workers, a suitably hawkish Sikh from the EEPTU (a very apt union for that fighting nation) and a gentle speaker from Bolton actually gave the Conference its only experience of feeling, and deserving to feel, good. There were lucid intervals of course, notably a grown-up's contribution on the Economy from Roy Hattersley, the best thing he had done for a year. But this was the Conference that took Arthur Scargill to its heart. Never mind the marbles fired from catapults or the fifty-one stitches in the face of a working miner, or the half-bricks through windows by a picket force happily kept trembling on the edge of grievous bodily harm. The Conference wanted real leadership, the rejection of 'Tory laws' as not being fit to keep, the endorsement of physical-force trade unionism – Feargus O'Connor without the charm – and all the sheer, sweet, concentrated rage that Mr Scargill manages to embody. As somebody once remarked of Wagner, 'It isn't all that bad, it just seems that way.' *The Twilight of the Gods*, or *The Twilight of the Accredited Delegates in Good Standing* is pretty much what we witnessed. Mr Kinnock became the prisoner on Tuesday of the ranting mood of Monday. He made therefore a speech, dexterous, evasive and submissive, in which particles of reservation were so skilfully secreted that the roaring activists missed them, but to which the recording media, who were excessively nice about it, could be directed. 'It is', said one of his aides, 'a much better speech when you *read* it than when you hear it.' The art of leadership in the Labour Party is thus one of not giving offence to the Party while smuggling small particles of sense on board for a private viewing by the cognoscenti. 'I am their leader. I must follow them.' The words attributed to Ledru-Rollin chasing a riot in 1949 are now the working practice of Ledru-Kinnock.

Not that we should blame him too much. Labour Conference has become quite frightening. Reminiscent of the old Glasgow Empire Theatre, where, it was said by artistes, 'If they liked you they let you live', and to which the shipyard workers would go on Saturday nights with pockets full of rivets to throw at the people they didn't like, Labour Conference has become a palace best approached with police protection. It was open to Mr Kinnock to speak from his heart, to be pro-miner and anti-Scargill, anti-Thatcher and pro the acceptance of law. He does not want for courage, and the Left knows very well what his position truly is; it detests him for it. But the Blackpool Conference was flooded, first with the rage of zealots, then with the fear of everybody else. The Conference was suddenly like a pit village on wheels and one learned quite what is meant by the term 'tightly knit communities' – places where people are terrified of stepping out of line.

As for the topic of Defence, that passed almost irenically, so entrenched and absolute is the unilateralist position. The winning side can afford to stay calm. Though 'calm' is a word in need of interpretation. One speaker, a Mr Burden, denounced 'our so-called allies, the US' and went on to sketch 'the American military establishment of gangsters'. 'Labour, said Miss Debbie Venn, was 'the living, breathing, caring party of life, not like the Tories who were the party of death'. Less overwrought and almost by way of light relief, Mr Wolf of Blyth announced that war was 'a class issue'. 'When was a war ever created by a member of the working class comrades?' he asked. Leaving aside Arthur Scargill, how about Mussolini, that Socialist blacksmith's son? Frankly the only good thing about the 1984 Conference was the absence of Clive Jenkins. Perhaps also a little credit should be given to the conduct of Alec Kitson who reminds one how pleasant old-fashioned Soviet-liners can be when compared to the eye-gouging dementia of the infantile condition. Mr Kitson contributed to serenity in this potentially violent debate (on Peace) with a speech of such stunning, specific and categorized tedium that one was tempted to call him the humane killer. Together with a fraternal delegate from the Co-operative party, Mrs Jessie Carnegie, who broke up the morning session, he stopped the natural hissing and spitting wrath of Mr Burden and Miss Venn dead in its anaesthetized tracks. What Captain Scargill had aroused within delegates Mr Kitson, in his civil but grinding recital of superfluous detail, reduced to passivity.

However, the talents of Alec Kitson to stop the Lebanese civil war notwithstanding, it was clear from the motions voted on that not only is unilateralism part of the landscape of Labour but that the Conference delegates showed a large majority keen to leave NATO. Whether they would actually have favoured joining what one press hand-out described as the Wallsall Pact, no one knows, for the cautious, good sense of the union block vote quietly offset the floor vote. Incidentally the delegates became very angry with Mr Gavin Laird for mentioning Soviet missiles and troops in Eastern Europe; not like the weapons of the American gangsters obviously – ballistics for the people! But the show of hands is on the record and it speaks with perfect fidelity for the delegates. This point has not been grasped clearly enough amid all the other debris of a suicidal conference. A neutralist majority exists on the floor; how long will it be denied logical conclusion? In 1984 we had Mr Healey in his less than endearing role of grand old loyalist saying to a press-garlanded Fabian meeting that he agreed with the new Defence policy 98 per cent, but surely we could be a tiny bit flexible about Polaris? By what percentage figure – 93 or as little as 89 per cent – he will agree when the Party goes neutral we shall see when it does.

The old Labour Right is in the paradoxical situation of winning allies within the Party and ceasing to exist. Mr Kinnock and his friends may be forced into alliance with the Hattersleys and Kaufmans of this world; he may find them more congenial company. He may in the process drive the editorialist of *Tribune* into fresh rages at a man whom he proclaims a seller-out. But the moderate option has gone for good. Healey is deluding himself; others, less sanguine, are simply motoring over the course. The 'class-conscious comrades', as they frequently described one another, have most and will soon have all of what they want. This Party has abandoned itself to routine hysteria. 'I know who the enemy is,' said one intense female delegate. She probably meant the Americans or the capitalists but she and Conference would have been happy to include Mr Healey and Mr Callaghan, who are, as she might put it, enemies of 'the Party's correct line'. With the Party's correct line who are they to argue?

The events of Brighton in October 1984 took us outside ordinary experience. The attempt by the IRA to murder the Cabinet with a bomb placed in the Grand Hotel, Brighton, followed a precedent set by the psychopathic regime of Communist North Korea whose bomb in Rangoon, Burma, succeeded in almost completely wiping out the delegation of South Korean senior ministers, but missing, very narrowly, President Chun of South Korea. The aboriginal mind of the Falls Road found similar expression. Like Mrs Thatcher, I was working late, on an article for the *Sunday Telegraph*; and by the oddest of ironies was just concluding with a passage on that day's delightful speech by Norman Tebbit when I heard a crumpling and unpleasant noise. For a short while I took it for some seaside upset, caused by what Mr Peter Morrison called, 'Bloody Young Conservatives', or alternatively a street lamp damaged by a high wind. Then I heard a voice shouting, 'A bomb's gone off in the Grand.'

The next few hours were a desperate mixture of sickness and exhilaration. Also one's mind does not work very clearly, precisely because the sequence of events is so aberrative; rather obvious and logical conclusions are not quickly grasped. A hotel with part of its front simply no longer there is such a surrealistic oddity that the necessary implications of very many dead is not quite comprehended. Everything is out of place: formal and rather correct ministers of this and that, with their shirts flapping; a crowd milling innocently and foolishly around, across road and pavements and back again; the television people with their little bits of instant verismo and their useful strong lights, snatching up scraps and pieces of news, and the news itself all broken jigsaw, like the fallen front of the Grand Hotel.

Where had the bomb gone off? Two witnesses, sitting late on the veranda, were sure it must have been in the foyer. 'There was', said Michael Fallon, 'a great whoosh as the dust and masonry swept through the front door.' But this didn't fit with the missing upper storeys of the hotel, so briefly a two-explosion theory grew up, approximately followed by police anxiety about a possible second device in the next-door Metropole, and by the immediate re-evacuation of those who had fled from the Grand to their neighbour out into the street again. Another rumour quite absurdly had it that the bomb had nothing to do with the Cabinet. The Iraqi Ambassador had been staying in the hotel. This explosion was the doing of the Iranians. After all an olive-skinned young man had been seen running away (presumably running like hell, a very natural reaction). Kept back from the Grand by police barricades, we were at first assured that all members of the Cabinet were safe, something that did not seem, even then, to be very likely.

My guess at that time, on the strength of the scooped-out fourth, fifth and sixth floors was that a dozen people must have died. (I reckoned without the superb structures of Victorian building methods: the technology of 1864 saved a good many lives that night.) However one could make one's own deductions. Any minister not present in the dishevelled democracy of a 3 am crisis was, unless otherwise accounted for, at risk, no matter how many assurances had been given. Now we know, while we stood in stupid impotence at the one end of the prom, which of the dead and living were being dug out. I had been talking with Norman Tebbit seven hours before. I had been writing about his speech when the bomb went off. Where was he? 'Not to worry,' said someone airily, 'He drove home last night.' Tragedy has a way of making idiots of us.

This was the conference to end conferences. They will never be the same again. That jolly piece of convenience and good company, the conference hotel, where the great ones accumulate for the lesser ones to mill around, is over. The Special Branch will have insisted on a diaspora, with ministers sprinkled around the town. Because a concealed long-term precision-fused bomb can go off anywhere, the social life, which is a big part of conference politics but which attracts concentrations of senior people to the most popular parties, will be under pressure. The *Blue Review* will be too dangerous, so will the Gordon Reece champagne fountain, the best party at all four conferences. We shall get our politics now *à l'Américaine*: a frozen-featured apparatus of pistol-carrying men will be everywhere and will govern what is done. Politics is likely to retreat behind a bullet-proof screen. Mrs Thatcher goes on about democracy but we shall have less of it. Police powers will expand to fill the hole blown open. It will not be effective surveillance against the next attack, but it will be surveillance all right, and the innocent generality of us will feel its fingers on our collar.

There is a whole separate world of Conservative Party Conference which it would have been pleasant otherwise to describe; Michael Heseltine in his best Huey Long style, the King Fisher soaring to heights and dipping to his familiar depths, appropriating the Arromanches ceremony for dead soldiers of the Normandy invasions for the sake of his own golden profile. There was Peter Walker selling policies off the back of a lorry, boasting about how much had been spent on the mining industry and how he would personally stand and fight against Mr Scargill. Perhaps he would, but reports of Mr Walker's desperate anxiety to quit the strike combined with other reports of his earlier insistence that the miners would not engage in a long strike or that they would soon go back had the effect, when coupled with other past promises from Mr Walker, of making his performance seem the purest toy theatre.

There was that delegate, Mrs Susan Gillies, who proclaimed that unemployment was best dealt with by small-scale endeavours. For example, people might go in 'for anything from singing telegrams to baking pâté for sale under contract to the local delicatessen'. Thus does Weybridge speak to Hebburn-on-Tyne! Add in the words of Heartless Nigel telling the delegates about virtuous American workers who went on strike *against* a pay increase, and with pâté-baking you can combine cotton-picking.

All these and many more were on display but it seems wrong to linger over them. Nothing is risible in the perspective of death. Mrs Thatcher chose to bid the Conference continue in order to concede nothing to the good Irish patriots. It was entirely understandable but, I think, a mistake. Normality cannot be resumed six hours after an attempt at mass murder, and one unlucky delegate proved this by not quite correcting his script from where it had stood on Thursday night so that, to his own horror, he found himself speaking of 'this splendid Conference'. The malign and hysterical words of Miss Debbie Venn at Blackpool the week before had become true in a perverse and absurd sense. 'The Tories', she had said, remember, 'are the party of death.'

In the presence of death the best you can say is nothing at all.

3

The Sunset Hooligans

Up the corridor and away from the structured tumult of the Commons Chamber lies the House of Lords. Decorated to the specifications of Augustus Pugin who, like Peacock's Mr Chainmail, believed that nothing good or true was created after the twelfth century, it is, for those who like that sort of thing, a splendid place. And Victorian bad taste having come thumping back into fashion, who has the nerve to say that it is not? Perhaps the friends of Lord Shinwell? That peer narrowly averted the most interesting political death in years by happening not to be in the Chamber at the moment when a roof boss of chaste design detached itself from the ceiling, to come hurtling down on his lordship's customary seat. Perhaps if the President of the Royal Institute of British Architects should be ennobled (an act against nature) the whole roof will fall in.

For those who cherish the aristocratic principle as this Cromwell-to-Bright republican does not, the prospect of dilution by merely meritable men has always seemed painful. The Lords, remember, threatened during 1910–11 to 'die in the last ditch' to resist abolition of their residual veto. They were coerced into surrender of that power, only by the threat of a mass creation of Liberal peerages, a thousand if necessary, coronets for the Edwardian equivalents of car salesmen, not to mention academics and novelists, even poets. Ironically that roll-call of talent without quarterings has long since passed into the Upper House; and if it had not gone the Lords would have died quietly after a long illness bravely born, in or about 1967. If we owe any debt to Mr Wedgwood Benn now chattering on the margins of rational discourse, it will be for his efforts in setting free those peers who wished to rejoin the Commons. But far more important than the thin trickle back to the commonality has been the Missouri-like flow of life peers into the Upper House.

Lord Willoughby de Broke who led the ditcher peers in the spirit of 'Let wealth and commerce, laws and learning die,/But leave us still our old Nobility' would not have cared for the class of person now taking his seat: Lord Rayner from retail trade, Lord Hanson from London Brick, Lady Cox from school teaching, Lord King from heavy engineering, Lord Bauer (the unflinching son of a Budapest bookie) from economics; and these are only the Conservatives. The Life Peerages Act, which looked at the time like a gimmick and may well have been meant as a gimmick, has actually matured, and its better effects are now being felt. There were, after all, two wrong paths available for the Lords to tread. Given ten years of Mr Heath (which would have had us worrying about bigger things than the Lords), the Chamber might have taken on full corporate form with the heads of industry and trade unions marking themselves off as an estate of the realm. Much more of Harold Wilson, a man of endearing frivolity in these matters, Lords Grade and Delfont might have been joined by the cast of a Gala night at the London Palladium. At Lord Frankie-Howerd, Lord Wogan and Baroness Rantzen the most demotic spirits might draw a line. After all, only a natural good taste prevented the former Ted Willis from taking the title Baron Zedcars.

What actually happens with the Lords is that the dafter nominations quietly fade into the background, saving the peerage for their letterheads but not troubling the legislature. But a variety of more or less expert people, many with an urge to communicate and instruct, has set about functioning busily as elders and betters, treating new-fashioned law like a dubious biblical text in need of revision. In straightforward debates, they assert their expertise to a forewarned press. Lord Carver is a good example, saying roughly what Marshal Ogarkov said in the Soviet Union, – too much duplication of nuclear weapons, not enough spent on the conventional front – but did so without being banished to a military academy in Carmarthenshire. The bishops too, having lost their original empire, have suddenly discovered a role; beneath lawn sleeves pectorals are rippled. The decent, commonplace Bishop of Durham is only the latest in a tradition of socially conscious, faintly swinging clergy to preach the gospel of Keynes crucified, in whose resurrection, above that of any other claimant, they seem to place most faith. All you can say is that it is better than having a sheaf of Rt. Revd. Collinses; we do in all conscience already have Lady Catherine de Burgh!

The other effect of the Life Peerages Act, one that has only slowly evolved, is the idea of active MPs of working age, unlucky in an Election and gearing themselves for ambitions not much above Minister of State, going cheerfully – well, quietly – to the Upper House. Significantly, Mr Michael Foot's too-soon-derided nominations, Albert Stallard, Ted Graham and David Stoddart, have all put in admirable peformances. Working Westminster politicians without *chic*, not stricken with the senescence common to many past ennoblings, they have carried on with the work that they did in the Commons, treating their lordships' chamber as the continuation of their political careers by other and less felicitous means.

The old curse of the Lords and the reason why it might well have died was old age among the membership. This together with hereditary exclusiveness, Conservative bias and knowledge that it had no influence, demoralized the House. It agreed with Conservative governments; it was terrified of Labour governments and was thus of no consequence to either. That grey nodding head would certainly have fallen beneath the blade of some meddling practitioner of the administrative baroque like Sir John Maude, the mandarin who helped Peter Walker turn local government into Sicilian layer cake. Incidentally the smooth, wrong Sir John finished as Lord Redcliffe-Maude. The House in which he took the prescriptive seat of the retiring office-captain has become a vastly more useful place for business than the metropolitan counties he created, and which their lordships temporarily rescued from peremptory oblivion. Unlike the institutions of 1974, the Lords is a classic piece of English muddle, compromise, and getting it right. The minds of tiresome men anxious to iron out anomalies have been exercised for years by the inconsistencies of the Lords' make-up. They neglect the inherent glory of anomaly. With the hobgoblin of administrative reform murmuring 'rational structure', 'sweeping away of archaic elements' in their ear, they fail to see that modest amendment will outlive and outperform packs and sects of exciting new structures. A metropolitan council stands in relation to the Lords rather like a high-rise, high-suicide council block with a jammed lift to a decently tidied-up Edwardian terrace with new plumbing.

The Lords works well today precisely because of its anomalies. There is a hereditary element decently doing its old-fashioned duty together with a flash new meritocracy of Quintons, Bauers, Beloffs, Lewins and Chapples. There is the ordinary provision of sunset homes for aged Cabinet Ministers. There is the new element of healthy middle-aged recruits from chance political defeat; and they seem all to rub along together surprisingly well. The touch of aspiration natural to a child of the Dukeries may have encouraged Mrs Thatcher in the odd new experiment of reviving the hereditary peerage ('first tried out, with her classical high caution, on a man with four daughters and on a bachelor). But that move is also a subtle compliment to the House itself. This is a club people *do* want to get into, and if possible put young Reggie down for.

The House of Lords has managed so well by not submitting to wholesale constitutional reorganization but by making piecemeal reform of itself. It has come usefully and thoughtfully alive. To take a single instance for which Harold Wilson deserves great credit, we now have a number of Black and Brown peers. The malignant Hilaire Belloc (whose recent biography reveals him to have been a moral contemporary of Julius Streicher) described in his verses about the peers a certain 'Lord Uncle Tom who made pronouncements of peculiar weight upon the cocoa trade'. What is attractive about the way in which the classic, abiding liberality of this country shrugs off the sentiments of Belloc, Carlyle or Evelyn Waugh, is that the Commonwealth peers, starting with David Pitt, seem to have acquired most of the amiable, gently bumbling qualities of any seventeenth baron who has owned bits of Shropshire since Henry VII. The good angel of Lord Emsworth still touches the Upper House, for all the crack regiments of intellect it has recruited.

No one of course more perfectly affects the Emsworth colours than Lord Whitelaw who, despite every sort of mishap, represents something vaguely attractive in English politics, though he is a terrible enemy to make. Not that the sight of Willie carrying a dead rabbit calling itself the Cap of Maintenance on the end of a sword during the State Opening, and watching it with all the subdued horror of a man who expects it to fall off, was not funny. But then the State Opening is pretty hilarious itself with royalty doing its ceremonial stopwatch job, as the Queen's Most Excellent Majesty times itself for an entry at 11.27 precisely, with everyone else walking backwards. It may be good for tourism but is it very grown up? And grown up, by and large, the Lords is.

The new value of the Second Chamber is that, despite minor eccentricities, it is a more normal place than the House of Commons. There is no Viscount Skinner, thank God, nor no Baron Nellist. The pages of ministerial speeches are not snatched and torn up; a mob of sullen sneering peers does not gather before the woolsack; in this House civility is king. 'I did think the views of the Noble Lord, Lord Snuggs, mistaken, if I may say so' is about the hottest thing you will hear said by way of dissent. This is a place to drive sub-editors and headline-writers out of their minds, uninhabitable places at the best of times. Their favourite words become unusable here: 'fury', 'uproar', 'lash', 'slam'. The primary colours favoured by our primitives have no application in an assembly so given to civil discourse. 'Peer expresses tentative reservation' is not going to wow them at the *Sun*; even my own *Daily Telegraph* likes a bit of shock horror on the side.

The nearest thing to horror to which their lordships' House can run is Lord Hatch of Lusby – tedious, sanctimonious and given to thinking in slogans as John Hatch and not discernibly improved by strawberry leaves. There is also Lord Jenkins of Putney, a former Minister for the Arts who looks hideously like a former Minister of the Arts, a snappish, self-righteous man with the look of having been handwoven by a somnambulist in a nightmare. There are metal-framed spectacles, a pursed little mouth surrounded by a groomed and preened little beard parted down the middle. The opinions remind me of an adolescent reader of Left Book publications whose mind has remained splendidly unamended, a schoolmaster Socialist of the kind that set Orwell's teeth on edge fifty years ago. Peace-marcher, protester, candidate – vegetarian and minder of other people's business, it is still right and proper that he should sit in the Lords. For he represents a body of men, recognizable by their sports coats, and over-exercised index fingers, which is of lamentable consequence in Britain – the pedagogical Left, George Weber without the crushed-beetle charm. With those two noble Lords no one competes, though the speeches of Lord Wedderburn of Charlton, legal adviser to the NUM, are the nearest thing to bagpipe music I have met in either chamber.

However the Opposition benches are impressive, despite this trio, and for reasons that would be instructive to the Lower House. Although there is no strength to match the present Shadow Cabinet, neither is there compulsion upon the Labour Leadership in the Lords to be jarringly partisan. The beauties of unelected life are apparent. With no reselection committee, no sponsoring union, no constituency GMC, the Upper House stands in relation to the lower for Labour men like a platform to a scaffold. The frantic desire to please disappears; the case can be put more quietly, but, most important of all, tacit alliance with the Independent benches and the (quite large) body o Alliance peers is accepted as a way of doing things; and, to the annoyance of the Government, it works.

The team led by Lord Cledwyn (formerly Cledwyn Hughes Chairman of the Labour Party in the Commons) indulges in littl of the mellifluous bombast that characterizes Mr Kinnock an Mr Hattersley, but it wins more divisions. The mere fact tha the Lords has been on the back burner for the media doe something to temper and make more persuasive the argumen used on all sides. Whether their lordships will survive th attentions of the zoom lens, with all it can do to bring out th orchidaceous vanity in any politician, is not yet apparen Clearly Lord Hailsham was defying decrepitude to be seen close profile and one has lived in hope that some of his earli not very *sotto voce* asides like 'Let's see how the buggers de with this one' would be caught by a stray microphone.

The strength of the Lords before the lens came into their liv was that they did a job, however unexciting most of the tim without the poses and grimaces by which politicians rattli sticks between their bars generally capture attention. Judgement must be reserved on the television experiment but it was a rich diet – swordfish cooked in papaw juice – for a distinctly convalescent stomach.

The Lords had, however, made itself interesting long before television by being unpredictable. The whips in the Commons send out for a majority as you or I would order cod and chips twice. An exceptional issue like education grants, where the dull-minded greed of the middle class wailing for its demon subsidy, gave the acting Government Chief Whip there, John Cope, a very rough time, is exceptional indeed. But as a guiding principle, even when an embarrassment of seats makes rebellion tiresomely safe, what Mr Cope wants Mr Cope gets.

The Commons is a conduit of patronage, free trips, junior office and smiles full of exciting possibilities. The Lords disposes a mere handful of jobs and, as the former Lord Stansgate grasped, is a dead end for the more carnivorous politician hoping for the top or near it. Those who come do so for interest, a little money and at the request of a Chief Whip who is able *only* to request. Bertie Denham, the Conservative Chief Whip, is probably as good at that job as anyone ever will be. Whatever can be done by polite insistence, discreet intimations that the-party-could-be-in-a-bit-of-a-hole-on-Tuesday-week-George-and-that-though-you-*are*-busy-with-the-winter-wheat-that-one-vote-just-might-make-the-difference, Lord Denham does it. Peremptory requisition is simply not open to him. He is doing, for all that the Conservatives look so strong in the Lords, a quite different sort of job to Mr Cope.

No punishments are available. It is counter-productive to withdraw the whip since this runs against the free, dare one say republican, nature of their Lordships' House. Republican it is in a way, because the Lords today has more in common with either of the two Houses of the US Congress than it has with the Commons. The little matter of needing to be elected again every two or six years still supervenes, but the same freedom of manoeuvre is there, the party divisions are marked out by the same plywood hurdles instead of the electrified *chevaux de frise* plus alsatians which separate man from man in the Commons.

The Lords is also more responsive to a public mood, hence Mr Livingstone's triumph. It has to be more than symbolic that a

House that behaved like a screaming boatful of Auberon Waughs when its privileges were reduced in the Parliament Bill should now be blowing kisses to the amiable Trotskyite across the river. After all, what Mrs Thatcher proposed for the GLC was a more drastic version, in the sense that hanging is more drastic than imprisonment, of Asquith's reform of their own House. Fellow feeling against constitutional draftsmen must have joined hands with a dislike of the lady's autocratic impulse to replace a form of elected government by a string of nominated committees. (Though what is the upper house if not a nominated committee? To be precise, it is a quango tempered by primogeniture.) Without lingering on a matter touched upon elsewhere, this was a good moment, despite the excesses of Mr Livingstone and the full horror of Mr Heath denouncing centralization.

The Government *was* peremptory; it *did* push its legal position in a way that is not good for pluralism, something Mrs Thatcher goes on about but does not altogether enjoy. Somebody had to be difficult; their Lordships were, and rose in most people's estimate.

Not that they confine themselves to defeating the Government only once or on a great issue. A total of sixty-five defeats have been inflicted on Mrs Thatcher's Administration since 1979 and they have run from Rural Transport to the Bar-tailed Godwit (another case of Emsworth striking again).

The most instructive expert on the mechanics and psychology of the House of Lords is my gifted colleague on the *Daily Telegraph*, Godfrey Barker, who has taken the Lords to his heart; and to him I am indebted for much essential detail. As Barker has pointed out, the problem facing Lord Denham is that his nominal Conservative majority contains a very high proportion of inactive peers, lost to sileage, stately-home administration or beyond the reach of the most persuasive whip, in the role of sheep farmers in Australia. The Labour Party in the Lords can and does run a tighter whip for all the freedom that is enjoyed. Most of *its* members are professional politicians, or at the least very keen amateurs. Lord Ponsonby (remembered by us former Fabians as the Hon. Tom Pon) managed on two key votes in April and June 1984 to put up 66 and 85 per cent respectively of his maximum vote (85 and 109 out of 128). The Tories, running very hard and pulling out both the *bombard* and the *vox humana* of the Chief Whip's available organ stops, managed a constant 56 per cent (213 and 214 respectively from a theoretical 381). Both votes were won but, given good turn-outs by the Alliance and crossbenchers against the Government, plus Bishops and cross-voting Tories, the Conservative Chief Whip can take nothing for granted; nor does he.

His 56 per cent turn-out was the product of one of the very few three-line whips issued. These are employed sparingly in the fear of diminishing returns. There is no point in withdrawing the whip since the man involved, having nothing to fear or hope for in the first place, either marches off home putting Lord Denham one vote down, or, getting thoroughly annoyed, he stays to vote regularly with the Opposition putting him two down. A sensible man, Bertie Denham never does withdraw the whip (though he relented and made an exception for Lord Alport); he adjusts to the inherently free spirit of the place by efficient civility, getting the vote by reasoned request and occasional summoning up of his territorial reserve.

Both parties are buoyed up by a daily stipend of £61 for all daily attendances of peers (something whose importance their lordships do not care to stress but which, compared to the receipts of most other pensioners, looks rather well). Quite how far this mild lubrication has affected voting patterns and in the favour of which party is an unanswered question but one worth asking.

For Baron Hardup the money must be very sweet indeed and even to the comfortably placed living in London and claiming no 'night subsistence', the residual £18 a day, if neither so deep as a well nor so wide as a Fleet Street expense sheet, will suffice. The total expenses bill in a steady week will not be much under £75,000. It keeps the numbers up, but as both parties have their share of needy and deserving peers, it is not certain which benefits most.

The real truth about the Lords has nothing to do with money though. Housman referred to death as an egalitarian, rather left-wing sort of condition:

> The brisk fond lackey to fetch and carry
> The true fond-hearted slave
> Expect not him in the just city
> And free land of the grave.

In many ways the House of Lords, where ambition is either fulfilled or beyond reach, a place where good politicians go before they die, does something to anticipate the great republic of oblivion. It is freer because it matters less, because all but a handful of aspirants to marginal minor office have no motive to be lackeys. Party loyalty subsists, but it is not spiked with the anticipation of office. The great well of patronage is down to the odd half-bucketful here. It is the most savage of ironies that the entire British system, which rests upon expectation, sycophancy and the retailing of honours, should actually come nearest to breaking down after the honours have been awarded. Hope is more useful to whips than gratitude. I am sorry to insist on throwing the English poets about, but really the Lords is rather like Keats on sex.

> Ay, in the very temple of delight
> Veil'd Melancholy has her sovran shrine.

Faced with a preponderantly nominated quango that behaves with the political fluidity of the US Congress, the Government Front Bench is required to be more persuasive than is necessary down the corridor. And here is one of the Government's problems. They have a thin Front Bench. Legislation dependent on Lord Belstead and Lord Glenarthur does very well to pass. Lord Bellwin, a local-government specialist from Leeds City Council called up to present the GLC nightmare, turned out to be as pedestrian and uninteresting in an expert way as any hereditary peer. Lord Gowrie, poet and idiosyncrat, has been a plus starting with the Arts, a modest homestead on the prairie of government; Lady Young is very much the Lynda Chalker of the armigerous classes, useful to have around but something less than a multiple-targeted warhead. Ministries of state were handed round in the early days of the Thatcher Administration to amiable but hardly percussive peers, like Lords Ferrers and Mansfield; individual hereditary peers like Anthony Eden's polite, serious son, Lord Avon, put their heads down and achieve junior office, but not even the fervent admirers of the Lords would claim that the Lord Whitelaw's team in the Lords is strong.

The accretion of David Young from the Manpower Services Commission will bring talent, but more is needed. As it is, the Government relies heavily on non-members of the Government.

A clutch of truculent Conservative academics like Lord Thomas (slayer of the little dragon, Alfred Sherman, at the Centre for Policy Studies), Lord Beloff, a short-tempered former Oxford professor, and the more serene Lord Quinton, Oxford in a good mood, all make contributions; but the Government is equally liable to find automatic ennoblements like Lord Carver and Lord Lewin, either attacking its defence policy in the first case or preoccupied with denying the war crimes of his Service in the second. The most recent Conservative recruits from the Commons are a thoroughly undistinguished bunch. The former Anthony Royle, elegantly described by Andrew Roth as 'seat-neglectful' in his time at Richmond, Surrey, can as Lord Fanshawe (Fanshawe!) lounge at ease; Sir Derek Walker-Smith was the most pompous and prolix Member of the Commons; as Lord Broxbourne he will not grow more terse. John Peyton was a combative little mannerist in the other place but, thin though it is, he probably represents the best Tory talent recruited from the Commons lately.

One of the likely long-term consequences of the new rebelliousness may be a revision of patronage practice. If the Lords is able to assert itself as a political fighting ship of the Constitution periodically turning a broadside on the Cabinet, then it cannot be used in the Honours List as a hulk in which to deposit hack, over-age politicians. Ironically, the defender of elected local government may find that the nominations upon which its own vigour depends will be scrutinized with a sharper, less politically easy-going eye than in the past. If I were in the prophecy business I would say look out for Mrs Thatcher learning at the knee of Michael Foot and sending more middle-ability men not yet devoid of expectations and in their early fifties, to the Lords. Not only will they perform better, but they will still be hungry.

An ironic side effect of all this independence of mind and of the sudden fashionability of the Upper House may be a further quiet dilution of the present inheriting peers. If they are reluctant as a stage army, more subordinable walkers-on may be found. The possibilities for future ill-natured relations between the Prime Minister and her Upper House are extensive. Oliver Cromwell, with whom the lady has a thing or two in common, called difficult MPs 'malignants' before purging them.

On the other hand, England being England, always look for the barley sugar rather than the baseball bat. No doubt, in re-establishing hereditary peers, Mrs Thatcher was doing no more than express her own regrettable spirit of social aspiration, but it was also a gesture to the Upper House, whose every expectation until the last few years had been one of the *diminuendo*. She not only paid a graceful compliment (which got her nowhere in the summer of '84) but she also armed herself with an item of patronage to keep Tory life peers sweet and perhaps Alliance nominations discreetly away at useful times. 'Might be able to get a conversion to something permanent for you, old boy' is not an argument marshalled at present but, in a country as full of Gothic notions of precedence as this, it would be unlikely not to have crossed the mind of authority. The House of Lords is the creation of that mild corruption which keeps the Commons relatively stable on the Tory side. But having been corrupted, their lordships have proceeded to behave in a thoroughly upright and independent way, not at all what was intended. With the hereditary element not much can be done, but the notion of freehold conversion will be a useful device to dangle over more independent spirits among the life barons. A guiding principle in politics is to find a low motive and satisfy it.

However, until some satisfactory form of political *douceur* is dreamt up (more peers will surely be going on overseas delegations in the future), we should take a mild pleasure in the fact that the Prime Minister is obliged to run a system with glitches in it. The Commons, always careful, has made only one substantial rebellion – on the sacred duty of the taxpayer to subsidize the university education of the children of rich parents, especially rich parents sitting in the Commons. The Lords by contrast has made a regular creditable nuisance of itself to a Government often right but very little checked. It is not necessary to have any time at all for the toadying impulse that finds the aristocratic principle so attractive, to see that in a rough, empirical way our present Upper Chamber has struck a balance between strength and discretion. It has come alive constitutionally rather like the baronets in *Ruddigore* stepping out of their picture frames, it has done so precisely because no tedious commission sat and reported. The House itself had travelled without knowing where it was going and has begun to work. It can look at the toy assembly in Alsace-Lorraine – prideless and functionless, an elective intestine, eating, drinking, sulking and collecting its gross rewards – with the quiet disdain of a working section of a real parliament. The House of Lords is a stone in Maggie's shoe, a series of divisions that the news media watch out for, a revisor and occasional initiator of law, a true part of parliament.

Above all, in a period of extremely weak, almost *pro forma* opposition, with a Government majority so large as to set peremptory fingers drumming, it has intervened on its own judgement against the party that the preponderance of its members support. Whatever its faults and eccentricities, it is an unservile House. Who would have expected to be able to say so much?

4

Cuddly, Cute . . . and Dangerous

With the newcomers into the Commons we have problems. The Conservatives, having won themselves a majority which would make up half the crowd at one of the less well-attended Fourth Division grounds, their backbenchers can hardly complain if they are occasionally treated as £10-a-day extras hired by a film company from the Mexican Army. It may not be the way they see themselves; it is the way they are seen. They are the victims of crowding out. The Speaker, who takes a great deal of minute trouble to be fair, though he is not helped by a defective computer which records unsuccessful attempts at intervention as full-dress speeches, is conscious that the ratio of speaking chances for a Social Democrat to a Conservative is on the scale of about five to one. The 395 cannot hope to be as well accommodated as the 7. Accordingly, much talent has to be judged so short a distance into a parliament on private contracts and general reputation. It is liable to revision as this flotilla, keeping close together, moves out of coastal waters and some of its number hit the Dogger Bank.

Firstly we might give attention to the Tories' only pit village, a tightly knit community of formidable, often St Andrews-schooled, classical economists. Peter Lilley, Christopher Chope, Ian Twinn and Robert Jones represent a good deal of talent and they have the same effect on your slow-minded traditional Tory as hydrocyanic acid. One lapel-seizing aldermanic elder remarked that he did not recognize them as Conservatives. This flattering view reflects a seriousness, a set of firm views and what is resentfully called ideology. They are the results of an intellectual tendency (there is no other word for it) created by Hayek, Friedman, the Institute for Economic Affairs and the Adam Smith Institute. They are in the tradition of Cobden and Peel – in historical terms, of classical Liberalism. Hardly any of them could be described as being right wing. The chemical formula of physical and terminal punishment, Ministry of Defence overspending and dislike of immigrants, which used to get such outings at Party Conference, has little or nothing to do with them. Their faults are quite mild, a certain excessiveness at worst. They like to write pamphlets and are ardent study-groupers, something that can make them boring, though the greatest distinction that can be made between serious people is the one that runs, 'X is boring, but Y is a bore.' The nearest of this group to the Y category is Christopher Chope whose carrying voice does not seem so well suited for local government, his speciality, as for ante-post bookmaking. A little of Mr Chope goes everywhere.

Peter Lilley is the obvious star of the group. a stockbroker-intellectual (not a happy thought); somewhat sub-glacial in manner, dry as dry and part of the Saharan mafia on economics, he was one of the first two 1983 entrants to be wanted as a sunbeam by the whips (PPS, while that Minister lasted, to Lord Bellwin). Lilley is looked up to by the others, feared by the wets but is reasonably free from gratuitous enemy-making. This is not the case with Robert Jones. His sardonic corner-of-the-mouth sectarianism in a Conference speech at the expense of Edward Heath, put him on to the 'discourage' lists of all sorts of people well placed to discourage. In his slightly grim way Jones can actually be very funny, something that seems odd in a Boyson disciple who does extra constituency canvases *outside* Election time on the float of a friendly milkman in Hemel Hempstead. He will be a superb constituency MP if you like that sort of thing. He is also a liberal on social issues; faced with a coloured candidate, Paul Boateng, for the West Herts seat, he gave sulphurous warnings against the minutest attempt even passively to take advantage of whatever feeling there might be on that count and devoted himself to beating up Mr Boateng's career at the Court of Ken Livingstone. Jones, although decently

ambitious and a busy committee attender, could develop, especially if the Party swung back to its spongy old orthodoxies, into
a Mark 2 version of the superb Nicholas Budgen, a pertinacious
asker of very nearly unanswerable questions.

Marion Roe, an associate friend of the group, has attracted
less attention than any of the incoming women but she has
amassed a great deal of unglamorous expertise of which
perceptive whips are likely to take note. She is probably the
ablest of the female intake, modest as that is. I would rate her
chances for office above the strenuous lady from Belper,
Edwina Currie. It is not that I personally dislike Mrs Currie.
She has, after all, a personality and not altogether an
unpleasant one. Among a batch of politicians who seem to
have had a small operation like a tonsilectomy for identity
removal, she is a sparkler among widgets. But she does, in her
bright, thick-skinned, tact-free way, make other people take
very deep breaths and start counting up to ten. The episode of
the handcuffs waved over her head, the television-covered trip
on a day in her busy imperceptive life, and a way of talking to
the press like a marchioness (though what is the point of
women in politics if not to let them play at being
marchionesses?) have done her very little good. I do know one
scrupulous new Member who argues that her intelligence and
originality outweigh the naive brightness and microphone-
hogging, and who generously says that her publicity success
should not be resented. He is right, but it is. A final point about
Mrs Currie is that she is altogether too attractive. That has
hardly ever been a problem with women in the Commons
before.

Not generally thought of in *that* light is Michael Fallon who
has been mentioned elsewhere but who has made himself
immensely unpopular in the shortest possible period of time. It
is not that Fallon is expert, pompous, knowing and intolerably
self-assured; every leader-writers' conference contains one of
those; but he was not wise to tell a senior colleague that he
would report him to the whips for a trivial irregularity. Oswald
O'Brien, the Labour MP defeated by Fallon, has many Tory
well-wishers. This young man has something deficient in his
cold personality, a sort of autism that makes him seem self-
preoccupied and carnivorous even to other politicians. Given

that he is both a good mind and a hard worker there may be prayers for character reform which will make him fit to know, but expectations are not high. The waistcoat is the man. Fallon is a talented aberration from the human race, a sort of gibbet, an accelerated sticky end to warn those tempted to similar courses of the terrible things that can happen to them.

There are others of a flash tendency besides Currie and Fallon. Robert Jackson has returned from Strasburg with arguably too good an opinion of himself and the bad habits of the late-entering quasi-senior type of civil servant turned to politics. He comes from the passionate-European corner as a former assistant to Lord Soames, and has, despite his polished civility, the essential qualities of the Foreign Office-and-Europe caste. He rather obviously strikes a slightly more right-wing public style than that of the company in which he rose, but he is saved from magisterial pomposity by being clever enough to see it coming. However, Jackson, who with an All Souls and Oxford Union presidency background is potentially a star, charms this observer very tentatively. I have a high threshold for politicianly assurance but Robert Jackson can float close to it. But his formidable intelligence and extensive culture are not luxuries. He deserves a post. However, he is unwise to manicure his fingers in the Chamber. Should his career advance, the nail file will become as much a personal emblem as the comb once was to Dr Owen.

By contrast it is not easy to conjure up much regard for Roger King. There is something about Mr King's thin features as he tries to please with a notably hard-featured defence of the diminished rise in miners' benefits, dismally reminiscent of the Chief Weasel. Then there is Timothy Yeo, a facile performer at Question Time who has managed to make a name of sorts by working that mechanism but who, like all new Tories, struggles to be heard. He does well in a sense, making his own opportunities, strap-hanging from whatever headlines he can get. His cheerful cynicism I find rather endearing.

If this chapter sounds at times a trifle irritable, bear in mind that these people are not watched and listened to exclusively in the hope of finding fault. If observers grow prejudiced against them, the MPs concerned are the architects of their own ill-favour. What registers too often is a calculated, self-serving speech which conveys limitless, selfish aggression beneath the flowering (or drooping) words.

There are people in the Chamber who leave it awash with spilt *id*. Some at least have a certain self-knowledge. Gerry Malone, a bundle of self-doubt contradicted by truculent assertion, is better than those above. He is for one thing a perfectly honest wet. It may well be true that Malone has put his money on the internal opposition (and who knows may have been smart to do so) but such gambling involves a certain courage, though no one should doubt his profound commitment to getting on. Malone, though, is ill served by his physical appearance. He has very small eyes that, as they constantly swivel for a better view of the main chance, seem to be operating independently of one another. He is also a hard, combative, aggressive man temperamentally not equipped for the graceful side of politics. I like him but frankly he is not likeable.

The Labour intake, upon whom, after a run of the bleaker young acquisitors, we must take a rest, are fairly oppressive, but exception must be made for the excellent Stuart Bell. There is in Mr Bell, a rational, humane Geordie, speaking at all times as human being to human being, a very great comfort. In a happier Labour Party such men would have an inheritance and would be able to do something useful. The North East has not yet been taken over completely by the wailing little gremlins who rule constituency parties in great tracts of the country. Accordingly Bell was chosen and elected by Middlesbrough, just as the much frailer, more biddable Tony Blair represents Sedgefield (a seat abolished by the Boundary Commissioners last time but one, and with wonderful efficiency, re-created for the Election of 1983). Blair is a very nice boy, but he is political plywood. He is not sponsored by the General and Municipal Workers' Union but he has all the accommodating, losing-side qualities of Mr Basnett's dim little watercolour union. He will go as the wind listeth, protesting that he agrees with the wind.

Bell is not like that. He has an interesting, unorthodox background, a pit clerk, turned copy-taster, turned barrister (qualifying late and thus spared the personality disorder of the bone-bred barrister). Ironically for the point I am trying to make, he *is* sponsored by the General and Municipal, but unless I am badly wrong he will be a *Mensh*, much more likely to be chucked out or to go of his own accord than to be used as infantry in a bad cause. It is a melancholy prophecy to say of a new MP that he is more likely to go than be homogenized, but to such melancholy Labour has come. Bell is the old Northumberland and Durham right-wing Labour working-class tradition, made more sophisticated by a diversity of experience and education. He could be a very formidable figure on his merits but while the present Leadership will take him to its heart, he will be an anachronism in five years' time.

Representative figures of Labour's current *geist* would be Clare Short or Tony Banks. La Short has added a new terror to the afternoon. If one remains after the plastic toys of question time, Government statements and points of order have been put away, the debate that follows is usually a civil, reasoned sort of affair, little attended but no shame to the House that stages it. This is the non-newsworthy part of the day, which empties Chamber and Gallery but for which I have an affection. Unfortunately Clare Short, like a legislative gooseberry, stays too. The voice is high and intolerable in the class of the dreadful iron-corseted Mrs Kellet-Bowman among the Tory dead. But it is accompanied by trills of giggles and a Skinnerish disposition to make a running commentary on an unacceptable speech. Nothing can be done with the silly and immature Short until in the just course of time somebody hits her. Her husband, Alexander Lyon, is said to have given up Methodist local preaching to marry her. He would have been better off with local preaching.

Altogether more serious but no nicer is the man Banks. a *Nibelung* from County Hall of the sort Mr Livingstone keeps around him for the purpose of advantageous comparison. Banks, who sits beneath a side gallery slapping his knees with suppressed annoyance, has the odd, wizened look of an elf, as if he had wandered in from one of Tolkien's half-witted synthetic fables. Banks is the first of the GLC contingent to cross the river and, tribulation though he is, serves as a dreadful warning. In him venom, vitality, natural force of personality, the not negligible gift of contempt (none of the usual whining here) and a taste for single-handed combat run together in a personality cocktail with a sulphur base (better than some of the cyanide milk shakes sitting opposite anyway). If not altogether nice, Banks is at least candidly nasty.

David Nellist, who always sets me thinking about virtuoso performances on that little-exploited instrument, the nello, is in an altogether different class to Banks – a lower one. He was once observed before election to the House as a cheerleader, giving the beat to a claque of Militant Tenders. That is roughly his upper limit. Words and Nellist do not agree with one another; physical aggression of the sort offered to Norman Fowler's script are more natural. But when words *are* managed, they come out in a frightening, programmed, cybernetic sort of way. Poor Nellist, having very little to lose in the head anyway, appears to have been gutted, rewired and equipped with computer equipment of modest sophistication before plastic respray and release on to the market – like the Stepford Wives in Ira Levin's horror story. Nellist is too straightforwardly stupid to count as a horror story himself. The clichés of the Militant Tendency have the same range and repetitiveness as those of a retired brigadier in Staines or of the slow-minded, Bingo Little-style, City rich. We must look upon Nellist as the Toby Jessel of the workers' vanguard.

He may, however, have a slight intellectual edge on William Michie, the latest of the truly dreadful contingent of MPs representing Sheffield. A replacement for the amiable Frank Hooley, Michie is incomprehensible, as far left as his restrained understanding will carry him, and bears a resemblance to a man unlucky the night before in not finding a Rowton House. He is the sort of primitive infantry whom the Bankses marshal for their battles, not the new Model Army but the random levies they replaced – 'decayed tapsters and serving men out of a place'. Still, as any military man knows, much can be done with stupidity properly organized.

Since we are on to fools we should take a passing glance, as long we can stomach it, at Tory fools. The name of Bruinvels leaps to mind. This man made a shaming humiliated oaf of himself in a radio interview where he bungled the old chestnut whether a supporter of the death penalty would be willing to act as hangman himself by saying, 'yes.' (The correct answer of course is that that sort of thing is best left to a civil servant.) But what was worse than the blunder was the fact that Bruinvels didn't recognize it as one and was to be found at a reception the same evening talking proudly about his performance. Bruinvels, who despite unpleasant opinions is not particularly nasty, is simply a transferred research assistant. Secretaries at the Commons still forget to be properly respectful to the poor boy, remembering his days as a politician's runner. He means no harm; he is up at Question Time trumpeting the virtues of Government policy and telling us how small businessmen in Leicester are grateful for it. It is the price one pays for admitting adolescents into politics; they feel at home there.

Not worthy of attention but getting a little, is Phillip Oppenheim, 28 years old and now continuing his education at the public expense as MP for something called the Amber Valley (the Boundary Commissioners being incurable old romantics). Oppenheim has a gross thrusting conceit, which led to the issue of a synopsis of his young career and an offer, not I fear taken up, to supply his photograph free of charge. Imagine Edwina Currie without personality or intelligence and you have Mrs Oppenheim's boy.

A slightly more gifted fool is Keith Raffan, whose flight from the Press Gallery into obscurity is a bad precedent. I react to journalists in politics (and worse still politicians in journalism) like a citizen of the Orange Free State to a breach of the Immorality Act. These people have a wonderful sense of rhythm and many simple tribal virtues but they should not be taken advantage of, nor their flowers picked by the *Baasvolk*. Raffan has however a degree of natural inoffensive silliness that should enable him to merge happily with his surroundings. A man who was once at the centre of a Young Conservatives' fund-raising striptease can lose caste more easily than your ordinary Fleet Street drunk. Not much better is Jonathan Sayeed, the man who defeated Wedgie Benn in Bristol. Rather likeable than not, he is acutely naive and incoherent and he controls language like a defective sphincter. Still, he did a good brave deed (the shot fox is, of course, up and running) and one would vote for him in preference to Wedgwood Benn.

Not at all a fool, though likely to be underrated because he is speaking a second language, is Stefan Terlezki. His experiences of life have led him to certain simplicities of view about the Soviets, which just happen to be true. It is a small comfort to think that one of those Ukrainian refugees who might have been returned from Austria in 1945 to the mercy and quarter granted by J. V. Stalin should now be the Conservative MP for Cardiff West. When one listens to that gross old impostor, the Earl of Stockton, making lachrymose speeches about compassion in the House of Lords, it should be remembered that he has never denied the repeated allegations made by Nikolai Tolstoy and others that one man sharing responsibility for the despatch of prisoners into trucks at bayonet point for deportation was Harold Macmillan! 'Earl of Lienz' would have been a better title!

Excessively right-wing but not at all a fool is the brutal Terence Dicks, a man of Irish immigrant extraction who has played the anti-immigrant weapon like a political flick knife. Dicks in his Hillingdon Council days deposited vexatious Pakistani refugees on the Home Office doorstep. If his own logic had been applied to his ancestors, Dicks would be selling horses in County Sligo. However, he is enormously important in that he does come closer to representing the genuine fears and grim views of people to whom immigration has happened – transitively.

Life is not all as dismal as it seems at Westminster. There are decent and useful men among the intake. It is a real pleasure to see Bryan Gould back in Parliament. Labour on its present trajectory will not be commanding talents like this two elections from now. The TV annihilator of Francis Pym in the 1979 election, he has the gift of doing injury to the Government without raising his voice. As a don turned television reporter he is upmarket in his understanding, and blessedly terse in its exposition. A Gould question will be difficult; a Gould argument will have a sharp point with somebody on it. He is fighting below his weight in this place, having arts too subtle for the coarse requirements of a big political career. In a more melancholy way one might say the same of another re-entrant, Robin Corbett, descendant of the regicide Miles Corbett who in 1649 signed Charles Stuart's death warrant. Corbett is another journalist, an intelligence, a wry, sceptical sort of fellow who has been in and out of politics long enough to have very few illusions, least of all, I think, about the Labour Party. He is not so much Soft Left in his views as Posthumous Left. It is good to have him there but whether he sees himself as much more than a slightly scruffy ornamental duck on a stagnant pond is doubtful.

Much more surprising as a parliamentary asset has been Richard Tracey, the new Tory at Surbiton. Quite what one expected from a former radio announcer I am not sure, but the lovely-corpse experience of Tim Brinton had depressed the market. Tracey is neither an intellectual nor especially endearing, but as a creaturely footman he is a most intelligent user of question and of interjections in debate. He had had a number of minor successes and was already steadily building up a useful reputation when, against all the odds, he potted Dr John Cunningham, Labour's answer to the Annunciation. Dr Cunningham, it should be understood, since his Beowulf-like exploits with Grendal (and Grendal's mother) over the GLC, has become for Labour in their hard times a shining knight, a special hero, the Sir Percival of the municipalities. For Tracey to ask the simple question, 'Would he say if he would give an unequivocal pledge under a Labour government to restore the Metropolitan Counties?' was to bring the knight, clutching his throat in a death-gurgle, rolling from his saddle. Labour is in the business of being indignant about all Tory changes to local government but no more wants to pledge itself to restore the regional Strasburgs of no utility dreamt up in Mr Heath's time than does the Government. Accordingly Mr Cunningham was reduced to incoherence modified by jargon. Words came, meaning went. A backbencher capable of doing so much is like an anti-hunt protestor who brings down the Master of Foxhounds with an air-gun. Tracey has made a virtue of his limitations and is deploying them with the memorable economy they require.

There is a school of thought that thinks highly of Richard Ryder, the Prime Minister's former Secretary, and has all sorts of anticipatory plans for him, which will do him no good at all. He is quite simply the most diplomatic man I have ever met, oblique to the point of making all his points tangentially. He is certainly gifted; he is personally very likeable, but whether politics rather than a closed monastic order is his real vocation I am not sure. He is one of those people whose discretion is signified by ninety-second pauses (not in debate of course) while he thinks of the exact phrase for balancing civility with non-communication. Come to think of it, he may inherit the earth.

More combative and clearly shocked by his experiences of the Strasburg Assembly is Eric Forth, one of only two graduates of the Senate of Sibaris elected to Westminster in 1983. He adds some flavour to the thin broth of Scottish representation though, like most of the talented Scots, he sits for an English seat. He has impressed this observer as much as any of the entrants in the narrow field of debate and like many of the better, younger Tories has learned, at least stylistically, in the School of Tebbit; simpering is out! Another talent, but one very easily missed, is Robert Harvey, unexpected winner in a Welsh seat. Young, mild and – delightfully in a politician – shy, Harvey comes from the *Economist*, for whom he wrote the first-rate full-length survey of Italy not long before the Election. In fact, although his reticent style suggests an Englishman squared, Harvey is related to most of the Italian aristocracy, White and Black.*

Harvey is a humane, liberal-minded fellow who will count as something less than a natural adherent of Mrs Thatcher, but when tedious sectarian hats are off, he is one of her most useful recruits. His lack of aggression masks a very extensive grasp. He is far more promotable than most of the better-publicized names. Similar praise (and considerable affection is given by their colleagues to David Heathcoat Amory and Francis Maude, though candidly I have not seen enough to make a judgement. In the case of Mr Maude, the reason may be the sheer shock of finding the son of Angus to be like yoghurt to the palate after the cayenne of his father.

The Tory side inevitably contains people who did not expect to be there, including one or two who are less than pleased to find their career timetable wrecked by over-early election to a seat hard to hold next time while their local-business interests or professional careers are set back. Premature election can be very cruel. It is very easy to be in for a single term and then lose the seat with four and a half years lost on your outside professional ladder and never make it back. Some sympathy on these grounds may be owed to Peter Thurnham of Bolton; though Richard Ottaway, who astonishingly won the North Notts seat, has less occasion to worry. What a friend he has in Arthur.

---

* Not a racialist allusion; the Italian aristocracy divides between the original accepters of the Risorgimento and the Savoy monarchy (White) and diehard reactionaries like the Borghese who adhered to the unreformed papacy (Black).

Somehow I don't see Nottinghamshire voting Labour again for a generation after the Occupation.

Another unexpected but rather welcome figure is Cecil Franks who, to general amazement, defeated Albert Booth by seven votes in the un-Conservative town of Barrow. Mr Franks, with his sharp tongue, truculent nature and local-government expertise (he was Conservative Leader on Manchester City Council), is a gain, though because of illness we did not see much of him in the early months of this parliament. There is an intelligent cutting edge there; he will not make the Commons duller. If a minor *Daily Telegraph* prejudice may be excused, we have our hopes for David Harris, a product of the Alsatian Assembly, but more to the point a former *Daily Telegraph* political correspondent. As observed, the principle of political miscegenation is deeply regretted but it looks like a happy marriage and Mr Harris, with a dignity unnatural in the press, could pass for an MP anywhere.

As much could be said of the celebratory Nicholas Soames who, from being a pompous young man at Conference two or three years back, has matured into a sense of humour. He tells the story of an early pitch at an unwinnable seat in residual Glasgow. A fierce man came to the door of a tenement in singlet and trousers. 'Ah yes,' he said, 'I know all about you.' Now the Liberals, with their customary devotion to squeezing things in the scrum, had published a 'Society' picture of young Soames between chukkas at a polo match, leaning on his horse and swigging champagne from the bottle. 'Oh, er, er, I can explain,' he said. 'Dinna try, laddie. I've niver voted anything but Communist and Labour, but for you I'll give the Tories a go. You are interrrested in the twa things that interrrest me: horses and drink!' With so many members converted to Malvern water and computers, a touch of upper-class excess adds a little colour. Though one cannot help noting with the arrival not only of Mr Soames but of Mr Maude and Mr Heathcoat Amory that the Commons is keeping up its record for being as dynastic as any compositors' room in Fleet Street.

A word might be said at this stage for nice, unexceptional members, the link politics keeps with the human race. I offer Humfrey Malins, the good-natured, slightly fazed solicitor who did something for all of us by removing the unutterable Bill Pitt at Croydon. Also consider Gerry Bowden, an exceptionally likeable, self-mocking man not touched at any point by pomposity. Both take their jobs very seriously and themselves not at all. Either would make a good whip at some later stage, always providing that that office is not given over wholly to being a staff college for the High Command.

Finally the possible stars. Views vary on this one but there is little dispute about Michael Howard, who even managed to confect a defence for the freezing of capital receipts of local government, which made the last parliamentary Tuesday of 1984 feel for a little while like that day in Sarajevo. To add subtle argument to judicious loyalty at the very point where loyalty was in a seller's market was most accomplished. It is hard to see Mr Howard, whose dark angularity sticks out like a spare pencil, going anywhere but up. A slight difficulty exists for Colin Moynihan, since he represents a seat in Lewisham not well regarded by the actuaries. He is anyway so depressingly young that a period for relaunch can be afforded, but with a first-rate business career, high academic credentials and the most entertaining conversational style of all the new men, he must be part of future speculation. Rather to my own surprise, given some faint prejudice against the Foreign Office, I find myself admiring and wholly liking the new member for Buckingham. George Walden, despite the drumroll from friendly sources that marked his entrance, which was calculated to get up a diversity of nostrils, is as good as they say he is, but very different. Wisely, he has abandoned the four-ale bar topic of foreign affairs and is turning himself into an educational specialist, furiously angry with the simple decay in competence among those who teach and run schools. It is the best issue for a formidable new member to address his mind to. There is no bottom to that sump, and educational resuscitation will preoccupy us until the end of the century and beyond.

Walden, despite a lugubrious resemblance to Geoffrey Palmer of *Fairly Secret Army*, has a great hold upon essentials. (He had halfway persuaded me by his abilities that a machine-gunner's view of the Foreign Office was inequitable and unfair until I met a senior member of Sir Geoffrey's office, and had my lack of faith restored). Walden admires the French, a common characteristic of that department, but unlike the usual vintage-fancying, civilization warbler who goes every year to the Charente to renew his contacts with higher things, he admires them for being accomplished, single-minded promoters of their own interest. That looks like the beginnings of understanding. There has always been a touch of cross-Channel Gaullism about Mrs Thatcher herself. If we could set about being as dedicated nationally to the great god, number one, as our unloving neighbours, there might be hope for us.

With all intakes there is a liquorice-allsort effect. Rogues, idiots, nice guys, charlatans, substantial talents, even a few stars, are on hand. It is by no means a bad intake though it is short on extremes. There are of course both hummingbirds and hyenas, but the parliamentary jungle has been replenished this time with solid, unsensational animals, chimps, wart-hogs and lesser created aspirants of a sort to keep the parliamentary zoologist steadily occupied for a long time to come.

5

Post-mortal Depression

The Labour Party, in Parliament and outside, has become a profoundly unhappy place. Decline and deterioration are symbolized in the grey, grim unreadable pages of the *New Statesman*, once gladly read by opponents, now picked up only penitentially by supporters. The last editor of the *New Statesman*, Bruce Page, by no means a man of the extreme Left, did something very emblematic in his brief, disastrous time there. He institutionalized long-windedness, represented in torpor-inducing reviews of extra length on matters of relevance. Relevance to the Left is what death was to Keats, a resonating preoccupation. It means in practice a long witter on the feminist issue, cloudy pages of rinsed-out sociology and contentious tabulated statistical detail of which a left-wing version of Patrick Jenkin would be proud. Only the genuine insights of an excellent parapsephologist, Peter Kellner, keep the covers apart for a little while.

I wince at the *New Statesman* because its new, humourless, intense and windy style epitomizes the sort of person now dominating the Labour Party.

Let us be entirely unfair and take the case of Mr Bob Clay. He represents in the far left-wing interest Sunderland North. Mr Clay is, like a good many more, a spray-on proletarian. He was educated at Bedford College, a minor public school in excellent repute and (almost) at Gonville and Caius College, Cambridge, where he did not quite obtain a degree. Plunging into the workers' cause Mr Clay found employment as a bus driver, long enough to say he had been a bus driver. He jumped through various left-wing, and of course relevant, hoops, casting off the stigma of gentle birth and rising by a sort of social back formation to a Labour seat. Symbolically he replaced Fred Willey, a man of no social connection who had used his time as a prisoner of war of the Germans to take an external degree and advance himself to the bar. What Mr Willey did used to be called with approval in working-class circles 'bettering oneself'; quite how one describes the process of confecting working-class origins in the way that other men post non-existent collateral is best left to Heaven.

Downward mobility has a quality of falseness about it, a touch of nursery-level exhibitionism, spilt adolescence, which it is worrying to see in a grown-up and slightly surprising in a legislator.

One cites this artifact, this Tom Keating of a worker, only to indicate what the Labour Party's leaders are up against. Never mind the aspirations of the workers, concentrate on the affectations of the small gentry. There is of course a long and honourable tradition running from Attlee of Haileybury to Meacher of Berkhamsted, of men with socially elevated schooling turning radical. But there is a world between such attitudes and the unacknowledged condescension of Mr Clay.

A rough guess at the Hard Left content of the PLP might be made from the occasion when he and Jeremy Corbyn stood together open-necked before the Speaker's table as tellers in the division against the latest suspension of Dennis Skinner. This rite is almost as sacred in its way as the State Opening of Parliament. The Labour Leadership abstained. Only the unofficial whip of the Hard Left functioned, and out of a parliamentary party of 206 there were 84 willing to be counted by these twain. The implication is that the old majority of moderates, even if you stretch it to what is called the Soft Left, has, in this, its political Massada, shrunk very small. Forty-one per cent obeyed the call of Clay and Corbyn. This is not a party that wants office. And as a number of Labour members will quietly tell you, it is not a party that should have office.

It is almost impossible to underestimate the depths to which Labour has fallen. They are a party with 8 million votes that

80

used to have 13 million. Flattered by 206 seats in Parliament, they are still less than a third of the House's membership. The chart of electoral performance is a slowed-down version of the share-rating of a great company in shuddering secular decline. All innovation has been refused except the wrong innovation; a succession of managing directors has made market confidence addresses to shareholders' meetings, a rights issue has been floated on a dry market desperate with liquidity problems. And, in a sort of frantic desolation, the Company has turned to the least credible whizz kid on the City pavements.

Mr Neil Kinnock has a dreadful inheritance but if it had been less dreadful Neil Kinnock wouldn't have got it. The leadership itself is the product of the 1981 constitutional amendment – a piece of Gothic to delight Burgess and Street. In a moment of absence of mind I personally favoured the candidacy of Mr Peter Shore – not fully realizing how comprehensively the new Conference-plus-unions-plus-Parliamentary Party requirements would exclude forever and forever any candidate not of the Left or of the Sham Left. The system elected what at the time was called 'the dream ticket' of Neil Kinnock and Roy Hattersley. And though the incapacity of the one and the strange debilitated lethargy of the other have intimated less dream than sleep, with such a combination they are stuck.

An immediate reaction to the election in October 1983 was to see Kinnock and Hattersley, in *Jungle Book* terms, as Mowgli and Baloo – an expression of the impetuosity of the one and the elder protective wisdom of the other. It hasn't quite worked out that way. Within days, still at Conference where the selection took place, Hattersley, at a public forum arranged on the Conference fringe, demonstrated that he and Kinnock were not in the same class. Where questions were crisply, factually and amusingly answered by number two, a vast windy thirty-minute oration was returned to a single query by number one. Kinnock has little to say, cannot shut up and is Leader of the Party. In a year it has grown boring to write about him – not that this will stop us. When his good nature, his excellent jokes, personal decency and stupefying verbosity have been recounted, what is there to say about him? He is almost the antithesis of those heavy legal technicians who occupy most of the Tory Front Bench. The Brittans, Jenkins, Howes and

Fowlers – long on detail, short on felicity – are at the opposite end of life from Kinnock.

They know the book and (with perhaps the exception of Norman Fowler) read it aloud. Kinnock scans few details, often getting them wrong. The denunciation of a takeover bid by Standard Telephone (an American company) for ICL, which Mrs Thatcher pointed out was not an American but a British company, is the sort of preparation or dependence on others which attracts sour comment and nervous defence. At first delightful, he grows tedious. Having felicity without substance, he is the political equivalent of an exclusive diet of ice-cream.

What is remarkable about him apart from these known, obvious things, obvious indeed before his selection? Well, he has a certain courage. His career benefited from something he could hardly have calculated as an advantage, firm opposition to the pet fallacy of the late seventies – devolution. The Scots marginally, the Welsh hugely, were to reject Mr Callaghan's constitutional Wendy House. Kinnock had been a categorical opponent in the days when little Strasburgs in Edinburgh and Cardiff were high chic.

Another point, his Leftism is of an oddly honourable if slightly jumbled kind. My impression is that he sees Arthur Scargill as a left Fascist, but quite understandably has not the superhuman nerve to go public with such views. He is an honest nuclear disarmer, uncluttered in his beliefs and not able to keep up serious dissimulation, hence his readiness to discard Polaris, that great standby of recent Labour Governments. Yet he is not a messianist. Buying the complete CND line is his only absolute amid the flowing words. He shows no flair for hatred, nor the odd aldermanic self-importance into which the far more complex Hattersley sometimes stumbles. Almost certainly he has self-doubt. He came up like Hurricane Neil but now rains very quietly. An ambitious wife, the patronage of the last Leader and a conference bent on avoiding the best, all projected him, perhaps against his long-term interests, into the leadership.

He expresses this doubt by barricading himself against his own limitations, conceding powers to a kitchen cabinet led by Mrs Patricia Hewitt. This lady, pretty in the manner of a pretty hatchet, has imposed a Berlin Wall in the outer office. MPs who had tolerable access to Jim Callaghan, easy contact with Harold

Wilson and who could wander in at will to talk to Michael Foot, now make application in the manner of humble persons at a Checkpoint. Indeed the unendearing term 'Checkpoint Pat' expresses a broad consensus of dislike among the bossed-about Parliamentary Party.

Finally, when he makes a stand against the Hard Left, Kinnock, like Foot, fights the wrong windmill. To make reselection of MPs optional when those intending to drive their member out will exercise precisely that option, was an extraordinarily small issue on which to make a federal case at the Party's Executive. It was not disastrous, like Foot's stand (and collapse) over Peter Tatchell, but it is quite without point. He will get his way and have a paper victory on such issues if he is lucky and suffer memorable humiliation if he is not.

However, he has one great political advantage if it is used intelligently – television. Mrs Thatcher's best friends would not call her screen presence much of a strength. Overcoached or overwrought, she whispers and rampages by fitful turn. Neil Kinnock, who when not talking too much talks well, has the conversational touch of that medium. Always best when he relaxes, he should avoid the long, solemn Burnett/Day Crown Derby dinner service encounter (like the rest of us). Little and often, not always on pure politics, letting his good nature get the better of his official standing should be the maxim. The last thing we need is a structured Neil Kinnock confected from above in the worst American image-beautician style. He needs, in the immortal words of his wife, to 'shut up'. For quantity control in this man operates as quality control because even his formal speeches begin well, falling apart only as they trundle on into explanation and the substitution of words for meaning. Leave him alone over the short period and his very endearing, relaxed and funny style can, at least on television, work very well.

Musical metaphors always suggest themselves here, and the man who survived the somersaulting of his car while listening to the Brahms First Symphony should beware of over-orchestration. Bagatelles, *Lieder* and *salon* pieces will give delight; the full-scale *durchkomponiert* opera and the rambling symphony will empty the halls. The early part of his leadership has been unsuccessful precisely because quantity control is *not* working.

Question Time has heard him say at length in his best barricades manner what might have been sweetly insinuated in a dozen words. But he has not been exactly slaughtered by Mrs Thatcher despite the superiority of her strenuous, unexceptional mind, because they tend to bring out the worst in one another on a reciprocal basis. Both lose control and tend to stand minutes on end, turn by turn with occasional riotous overlap, at the despatch box, he declaiming, she lecturing, both going on. During the famous August 1984 Adjournment debate Mrs Thatcher accused her opponent of 'spewing out statistics'. He is normally blameless in this respect, while the lady will tell you the price of whiting, seasonally adjusted at the drop of a correlate. While both can bore, she bores with authority. In fact the sudden production by Kinnock in that very debate of a file full of dull damaging facts lightly dressed in numbers – about productivity, trade in manufactured goods and other unpleasantly tangible things – was quite impressive. It was at least a departure from his three-decker Tin Ebenezer rhetoric. That always comes at you in waves, as detected by Professor Higgins in the manner of Alfred Doolittle: '"I'm willing to tell you, I'm wanting to tell you, I'm waiting to tell you." ". . . Sentimental rhetoric! that's the Welsh strain in him."' Kinnock orates in a style astonishingly close to that – prose layer cake sustained by reiteration – and it does not work. It is as out of date as Marshall Hall's throat spray. Human kind can take only so much peroration.

Yet Kinnock's obvious weakness as a speaker reflects his profounder problem as Leader of the Labour Party. Lack of collective confidence on the Front Bench is balanced by a noisy and rancorous nastiness from the Left. If the effect on the Leader is that in keeping up a front under such stress he talks too much and invests an excess of enthusiasm, his deputy has given the best impression of catalepsy since the darkest pages of Edgar Allan Poe. The reasons are not clear. Hattersley's shift of portfolio from Home Affairs to Treasury might have occasioned distracted preoccupation with a harder, more cerebral subject. But Hattersley isn't stupid. He is more capable of grasping a Treasury brief than many who have held the office. The one variant on his name that isn't remotely fair is 'Smattersley'. His opponent, Nigel Lawson, though intellectually distinguished, lacks all political finesse, and the fight between them was positively looked forward to like some fifteenth-century morality play: *The mightye battle betwixt Pryde and Righteousnesse*. But the Hattersley sanctimony works have been hit by industrial action; there are pickets on the gates, deliveries are not guaranteed and the export market has been injured by complaints about after-service. Old Roy is like Keats's knight at arms:

> Oh what can ail thee, Knight at arms
> Alone and palely loitering . . .

Admittedly the Home Office was his element. The sun did not go down on Roy's deep sense of moral outrage, his devotion to a multi-racial society and to every able-bodied ideal within a twelve-mile radius.

All we get now are perfunctory contributions which break up the rolling silences between them. Hattersley, the most bubbling man when up, the most tersely morose when down, has his problems, not the least of which is the Labour Party. He likes Europe, he likes America. He is not a crank. A working majority of his party respectively do not, do not and are. Arguably he has reached the conclusion that Labour is now a fringe with a party attached to it, but he was not perceptibly cheered up by improvements, for what they are worth, in the poll-ratings. Even Hattersley, whose child-like ambition does not mean the absence of *any* principle, cannot be happy with the things he is required to stand for. Just as he publicly made a candid reappraisal of the largely incredible economic policy that Foot had taken into the 1983 Election, so he also expressed a murmured unhappiness at the development of Labour Defence policy.

As this development takes the form of abolishing all nuclear defence, unhappy he might be. Roy has devoted the talents of a potential theologian of note to argument by residuum. Whatever had not expressly been thrown out was or might be still there for the purposes of hypothesis. And by these means he has always been able to argue that Labour's position, though clearly controversial, could be reconciled with the assumptions of the preponderantly governing, preponderantly in-this-world Labour Party with which he had worked since entering the House in 1964. This passion for wriggling brings Hattersley into a great deal of scorn from Tories and from the Hard Left who both point fingers at his increasingly melancholy head. He is, they both say, glad that they are not like such a man, a careerist. So he is, but not in a dishonourable or nasty way. He has always wanted very badly to succeed; he has lived a life of extraordinary vigour preoccupied with doing just that. But he is also a candid man, emotionally incapable of sustained deliberate, self-acknowledged deceit (which is not at all to say that he never fantasizes).

Two things have now come to a head which affect both characteristics. At the low level (where most of us make our rational calculations) the careerist in him will have done the three-party arithmetic and will see no *independent* future for a party down to 8 million votes. As an obsessive calculator on the back of envelopes he will understand that the odds on Labour coming back solo as the government next time are substantially less than not good.

At a different level he must feel almost no kinship at all with Mr Arthur Scargill, with the rabbiting abandon of the Nellists, Bankses, Flannerys, with any of the rubber-daggered Cascas of the Berliner Ensemble behind him. Other people from whom he does not seriously differ, whatever personal sunderings may have taken place, went away in 1981 to start another party. Rationally, Hattersley knew that gravity was against them, emotionally he did also have attachments to Labour through his own obligations and family. Rationally at least he must have been right. In the absence of PR the Alliance has only a handful of seats. And yet David Owen as joint Leader of 24 is enjoying every minute of life and scoring a great personal parliamentary success; as Deputy Leader of 206 Roy Hattersley looks like a banker who bought the Bolivian debt.

Incidentally Hattersley's attachment to the Labour Party is rooted in the City of Sheffield where both his late father and his mother had valuable careers of the old-fashioned Labour local-government sort. More than any city in Britain Sheffield is now in the hands of very peculiar people, whom the rough charm of their Leader, David Blunkett, barely disguises. At the parliamentary level, Joan Maynard, Richard Caborn, William Michie and Martin Flannery are a quite dreadful crew. (Only Dr Duffy survives as a moderate and he under the blade of reselection.) Fred Mulley was removed to make way for Richard Caborn; Frank Hooley, an excellent MP of Soft Left provenance, was mugged by the prowling deselectors to make way for William Michie, who has the distinct look of an unsympathetic Man Friday. Although Hattersley himself is safe in Birmingham, which avoids excess partly through the involvement with Labour of great numbers of upwardly mobile people from the Indian sub-continent (a good thesis subject there), he knows from his Sheffield connection the precise nature of what is going on. He exudes a mood of profound unhappiness. Career and principle conspire to tell him much the same thing. He is not going to be Leader of the Labour Party and the Labour Party is less and less worth leading.

Now I was tempted at the election of this dream ticket to press that metaphor of Mowgli and Baloo. It will be recalled that Mowgli was a lovable but impetuous youth plunged prematurely into a jungle full of unpromising people like Sher Khan the Tiger, and that the equally lovable Baloo the Bear – older, wiser, if rather flat-footed – extended fatherly protection. I would not contest the lovable nature of both of our heroes, but while Mowgli is indeed rash and impetuous, not to say gabby, Baloo has retired hurt. What is Mowgli to do alone in the jungle if Baloo is in a state of immobile depression?

One of the things a fully alerted bear might have done would have been to scotch the youngster's odd belief that unequivocal, down-the-line unilateral nuclear disarmament was good politics. The Conservatives, as Baloo well knows, have barely used the 'Surrender with Labour' card. In the last Election they had no need of it and anyway enough cloudy imprecision hung about that precipitous peak to make it look less Eiger-like. Hattersley's candour has never operated against maximum ambiguity where Labour's exact position was concerned. But he has some idea of the speeches about the absence of a Labour defence policy that Mr Norman Tebbit will be making as Conservative Party Chairman in the long run-up to the next General Election. As much as anybody does, Mr Norman Tebbit resembles Sher Khan, small-boy-eating Bengal Tiger (quite lovable tiger actually, but the point will be lost on Mowgli).

The film of *The Jungle Book* has a song about 'Bare Necessities' that one can hear Mr Tebbit quoting. Whatever may divide the

Conservatives – and on personalities and the Economy they can be quite unpleasant about one another – on a broad line about Defence they happily converge. Should the Economy remain in the spastic condition generally expected, they will have more reason to use this particular artillery. 'Britain's safer with the Conservatives: don't let Labour ruin it'. Or if we were feeling upmarket at the Brothers Saatchi: 'Do not go naked into that good night' or the message xenophobic, simplistic and true: 'Defend Britain: vote Conservative.'

It is odd to contrast Hattersley with Denis Healey, who ought on any reasonable expectation to have become Leader of the Party. He was passed over for a man with a fraction of his talent in 1980. In 1983 he did not even bother to run knowing that on such a course he wouldn't leave the starting gate. Yet Healey has not called it a day, not gone off to manage Consolidated Laminates or NATO. Nor has he written that work on the philosophy of art with which he has been threatening us.

'I just don't understand,' said one member of the present Cabinet, 'if it was me, I'd be gone, doing something interesting outside. Why does he linger on?' It could have been a pathetic episode, like those defeated MPs who are to be found on the terrace in summer with a sponsor, sniffing the lost ambience. That isn't quite Denis's way. His performances against poor Howe have not merely been brilliant, like God taking on Bishop Jenkins; they reduced one pre-eminent figure on the orthodox Heavy Left of the Party to the privately expressed regret that Denis Healey had not – on simple merit – been chosen leader.

The wave of misery that hit the 52-year-old Hattersley has had no effect on the 66-year-old Healey. For one thing he is a gross optimist; for another he enjoys the fight, which he doesn't take all that seriously. The Commons for him is the Oxford Union using real bullets. I am not complaining. In the Commons, where the acme of high performance is somebody like Norman Fowler being briskly proficient and with the flavour of Perspex, the man who can turn on the Prime Minister and Foreign Secretary and say, "Who is the Mephistopheles behind this shabby Faust? Why, the Catherine the Great of Finchley' gets my vote any time. Bishop Gardiner's sibylline deathbed words about having 'denied with Peter but not wept with Peter' fit Denis better than they did that Christian imam. Denis doesn't weep about anything, but he will deny, obfuscate, evade, equivocate, strangle his grandmother, not for any special personal advantage, not as a blind party man adjusting to the adjusted line, but for the sheer love of the game and in order to stay in it.

Neil Kinnock may feel the odd pang and suffer cruel comparisons, but from where he sits the presence of Denis Healey is all plus. Indeed, although it says differently on the record, he is still Labour's Deputy Leader – as he likes to say, in a position analogous with Mr Gromyko's, though heaven protect us from Gromyko's jokes. When the Labour Conference of 1983 gaily elected that 'dream ticket', when Kinnock himself offered the sweetest places to his young men, the future role of Healey as the one star in the Labour firmament that could be relied upon both to twinkle and shoot was not thought of. They would be in a miserable condition without him.

By contrast Peter Shore is not a happy man. As an individual he commands very great affection and respect. He remains the rational arguer of a case, the holder of principle. But his defeat under the new election rules was so gross, so insulting – not from malice but because third candidates were put out of mind – that he has inevitably lost face and suffered hurt. Neil Kinnock, who is not always permitted by his minders to be as generous to elder figures as would be attractive and wise, shifted him down from the Exchequer Shadow to Trade. That in itself was a bad move. Shore's command of detail would have balanced nicely the expert but politically club-footed Nigel Lawson. At Trade and Industry he had to argue with Norman Tebbit, which he did the wrong way, growing hot and indignant and getting the rough edge of that corrugated tongue. And now even that function has been withdrawn from him. I haven't really seen Peter Shore in full heart lately, solidly though he works. This isn't his sort of party either, deeply as he despises Thatcher and everything about her – not by any means a general rule on the Labour Right – but then Shore is a social-democratic Keynesian of earnest conviction. The old influence for good and decency remain but there is none of Healey's cheerfully irrational fervour for the game itself.

Already linked with the Old Guard is Gerald Kaufman, which for the day-before-yesterday's cheeky office boy must be miffing. I am sometimes tempted to be a reluctant bear of Kaufmans on that commodity future market we sometimes play in the Gallery. He has all the talent imaginable, and wit and culture, which seep in from outside politics. But he has two problems: contempt for fools and fools. The fools hoped to be rid of him by reselection process in his Manchester constituency. They were most awfully unwise to do so. For all his physical frailness Kaufman is the man most likely to bite the constituency dog. Possibly, but not more than possibly, he might simply turn away sorrowing like Eric Varley, who, as exclusively predicted in *The Senate of Lilliput*, with no constituency dispute, quietly walked away, not to a flash or vastly glamorous job but to something useful and productive in industry. But Gerald Kaufman, by universal guess the author of the observation that the last Election Manifesto was 'the longest suicide note ever penned', is not the man for going quietly.

The Tories get Kaufman very wrong. Because he plays the parliamentary game for all it is worth and inflicts a good deal of injury on them, most Conservatives get a little haughty and tend to use the word 'clever' about him in an offensive way. There is a streak of cynicism but, as in most decent men, the cynicism is on the surface. His revulsion at, and perception of, the shift into a coalition of Leftism and slatternliness is probably the most complete and cool-eyed on the Front Bench. But while he is around he means to do a good job carbonizing the Tories. He is something of a contract killer and very useful. He is, on balance, a better journalist than Hattersley. If politics should fail him he has somewhere to go. He might well go happily but he would be happier if he had inflicted some injury first. Although he actually has good relations with Kinnock, of whom he speaks affectionately, he belongs to an in-between group that came up in the wake of the old seventies Leadership but with seniority over the Leader and the young men elected to the Shadow Cabinet in October 1983. There are few people as unpleased with the world as passed-over middle management, and no one should underestimate the unsettling effect of the leadership's sudden flight across the decades.

The experience of being led by a man on the threshold of 70 liable to be photographed with dog and stick like one of the more endearing life assurance posters was followed by a leap across twenty-eight years. For a cricketer Mr Kinnock is mature; for a swimmer ancestral. For a politician leading his party, he is seizing power from the cradle. The rising generation of Conservatives from whom the next Leader will be chosen (sooner rather than later I sometimes feel, listening to Mrs Thatcher) are in their early fifties: 1931 was a good year. Kinnock's Shadow Cabinet, so far from having been thoughtfully laid down, contains great quantities of *heurige* – green wines, like Mr Cook and Mr Straw. The generation of Hattersley, Kaufman and the departed Eric Varley has been leapt lightly over, though in fairness only Hattersley had been seen as a prospective Leader.

Of the elders, John Smith deserves some attention. James Callaghan's Trade Minister is frequently described as the ablest man in the Labour Party. The connoisseurs take to him very much for sheer intelligence and grasp, and he has a Tory following. His home base has been oddly secure, for Scotland has been strangely tolerant in the matter of reselection.

Mildly overweight, beaming through black-framed spectacles, but able, I always feel, to stamp on the odd windpipe if required to, Smith ought logically to shadow the Chancellor. He is more intelligent than Hattersley, actually knows about the City and could give Nigel Lawson a terrible time, but such jobs are given out on political not merit grounds. Smith had Employment, an unpretentious little portfolio, before reclaiming Trade, which he had run in Office, and may look with some envy at the Tory way of promoting technicians and operatives. He is a better talent than either Brittan or Fowler – the best of these oil-rag men, and incomparably superior to Jenkin or Younger. Unlike all of them he is a strong, amusing personality edgily respected by both sides. But really quite what is he waiting for? And, indeed, will he wait all that long? Outside politics he could command six figures without getting strenuous. Nobody, says the cliché, is irreplaceable. Well, they have tried putting Hattersley in Smith's natural job and some doubt is now thrown on that particular theory. Hattersley, it was observed above, is not stupid. Smith is clever.

Here of course is an irony. You can lose a lot of money backing mere intelligence. Politics is not a meritocracy. If it were Healey would be Leader and Smith would be his Deputy. Both the casters of votes and the distributors of portfolios operate their own unacknowledged *nomenclatura*, consulting lists of men in each of a party's factions and their claims upon support. The less democratic Tory Party can afford technicians, though one devoutly wishes they would find some interesting ones; Neil Kinnock has to juggle much more. Accordingly he is landed with a Treasury spokesman who has made as much impact as a sucking pig. He has had to demote Shore and deny Smith thus running real risks of losing the services of both. It makes political sense and no other kind.

However, a certain setting of the teeth on edge of the middle generation was inevitable despite Kinnock's attempt to soothe such men. The irony of Labour's position is that at a time when, undrugged and abstemious, it is recording results at which the England cricketers would hang down their heads, it has, unlike that team, rather a lot of talent. The men who were elected to the Shadow Cabinet in October 1983 frequently carry sharp swords, though the glittering prizes may now be located mistily up-perspective. There is more forensic talent here, more flair for the Chamber, than you will find in Mrs Thatcher's Cabinet, which holds more boring, ill-articulated, enervating men than God can quite have intended.

There are those who make great claims for Jack Straw, who had made a forceful back-bench and junior impression. Concerning Straw, briefly a national figure as an LSE co-ordinator of protests in the idiot year 1968, the market would take a fairly cool view. Straws have moved lethargically, offering disappointing results despite favourable early reports. Avoid. He is too pedantic, too diffident and seems not to take himself altogether seriously. But there is a touch, in milder form, of Hattersley's Complaint, more than a hint that a routine is being gone through without high or serious expectations, for no tangible purpose. I would also draw the inference that some way along the line Straw has become less radical, less impressed by the shrivelled kingdom of a truly Socialist party, which he and the rest of the Left, after having long sought it, are now entering. In politics sixteen years is one hell of a long time.

Perhaps because he is a natural optimist, Donald Dewar, an old-time moderate who should find the present state of Labour unsupportable, is happy. Donald is however incurably good-natured, and would be determined to see the bright side of Parkhurst. Anyway, as the Scottish shadow, he has the advantage of being compared with Bruce Millan. It has been an excellent move, if you allow for the exuberance that carries him into untranslatable Glaswegian: 'He is a sleakit little man who shows no spirit, no smeddum.' The effect is very good. For the long querulous groan of Millan, to whom Dewar is privately and publicly devoted, has been substituted a joyful sort of skirling – it seems the best word for it – a noisy, high-speed, well-argued case, zestfully and delightedly put. Actually Donald Dewar, among the grim, crepuscular men who have done their sums and sit betwixt sedation and resentment on the Labour Front Bench, looks like a version of the H. M. Bateman cartoons: 'The Shadow Cabinet Minister who enjoyed himself'.

He is long and lean with the features of a kindly giraffe with an academic turn of mind. It would be an overstatement to say that he had managed to make Scottish questions and debates interesting, but that steep sisyphean road is definitely being attempted.

A degree of uncertainty surrounds Denzil Davies, who has effectively taken over the Defence portolio from John Silkin. Davies, despite elaborate academic credentials, is one of those politicians who are advanced by a change of line. Defence has never been a favoured activity for Labour MPs. The Shadow Defence Minister is a sort of nightsoil man, necessary but not the centre of social activity. As the Party shifted to unequivocal unilateralism, one spokesman, Brynmor John, jumped or was pushed; John Silkin, who classes as a link between unilateralism and the Navy, held the job for a while and indeed continues in a vague co-ordinating position, a sort of posthumous shadow of Sir Thomas Inskip. Davies, once seen as a man of commanding insufficiency, is the principal spokesman. He is a slightly grubby-looking figure whom one instinctively wants to hose down, speaking with a Welsh accent not of the caressing, seductive Jim Griffiths, Nye Bevan, indeed Neil Kinnock, sort, but an 'indeed-to-goodness' Fluellenish kind that might properly come from a Welsh pony or a pantomine horse. But, in fits and starts, he has shown brilliance, notably in his recital of the catalogue of ministerial perjury over the *Belgrano*; he has outperformed expectations. Labour has some notion of the prospective unpopularity of its strip-club Defence policy and was happy to trust it to a figure who, it was hoped, would keep it in decent obscurity. He has let them down.

The find of the season, however, is Jack Cunningham, though any man put up to deal with the GLC Paving Bill would have been worth a twenty-point jump in the market. Even so Cunningham has made himself in a session. He is distinguished from a lot of front-bench frustration by courtesy, which makes him twice as effective in argument. Neil Kinnock himself is a gentle and humane fellow with no malice against his opponents, but he feels the need to shout and thump and generally to obscure his sweetness in the contest with Mrs Thatcher who has made some effort to obscure hers.

Cunningham, however, up against Patrick Jenkin, victim of a thousand knocks but also himself a model of civility, sticks to the details and works quietly and humorously to make the intelligent case that Government Members will grudgingly admire. His voice has something to do with it: a melodious mid-Durham soothed throughout by the Ph. D.-obtaining process. Cunningham is a dynast, the son of Alderman Andrew Cunningham who ran County Durham in a way that though it grew perilous and disreputable at the end, was not overall unenlightened. The young Cunningham is a product of the same union as his father, the limply meritable General and Municipal Workers' Union. And here is an irony; Cunningham is precisely the sort of second-generation, highly educated, moderate Labour politician who would have been predicted as part of a likely future in Labour's best days. And here he is actually ready and functioning as the enforced ally of Mr Ken Livingstone.

Never mind for a moment the unwise mechanism of a nominated quango used by Patrick Jenkin to mop up the GLC's superfluous year before dissolution. Municipal Socialism, to which Cunningham is literally an heir, has gone through a long process of deterioration, some of it Conservative-inspired – too much money, too little internal control, ugly concentrations of unchecked and arbitrary power. Finally, but only at this late stage, play-group Leftists have emerged who declare nuclear-free zones, allocate lesbian day centres, offer to negotiate with the IRA, attempt in Edinburgh to render that city's Festival ideologically sound, and whose conduct in certain council chambers has about it a touch of the Reichstag. What in the name of reason is Dr Cunningham doing in such company?

The answers to that unkind question lie in the decay of local government (a whole separate subject) – and in the decay of the Labour Party. A more political Minister than Jenkin would have strayed from the narrow brief to substitute a committee for a council and lingered long upon that decline of local government into something not now trusted with its own rattle.

In the absence of such reflective thinking, the debate concerned only the mechanics, which were bad, clumsy and peremptory. Accordingly Cunningham did an elegant job against the Minister, one that was grievously injurious to the Government and got its reward in the House of Lords. Soft-spoken, reasoned and persuasive, it rang bells all over the Government benches not merely with the embittered element coagulated around Mr Geoffrey Rippon, once the youngest ever Mayor of Surbiton.

No triumphs quite so remarkable have come the way of another new member of the Shadow Cabinet, Giles Radice, if only because the Education Secretary, Sir Keith Joseph, is a difficult man, in that post for any reformer to attack. But Radice, apart from the single episode of university grants, has performed with perfect respectability and competence. The heir of radical Lombards who fled the rule of Metternich in northern Italy, he is now confronted with Mrs Metternich and is a trifle perplexed. The old saying was *Il Inglese Italianato è diabello incarnato*. Looking at Giles and listening to him I would say that *Il Italiano Inglesato è l'uomo moderato*. He is upper class (Winchester and New) in the inoffensive way of William Whitelaw. As with Cunningham there is a hint of a time warp. This is the sort of clever, reasoned, fair-minded, likeable chap who belongs morally and temperamentally in Hugh Gaitskell's Labour Party. The gifted and privileged commonly came into the Party at that time (Shirley Williams, Dick Taverne, David Owen); they had a loose common cause with trade-union moderates and sound municipal men. It was an honourable alliance and a highly electable one, but it has gone to hell in constituencies and conferences over the last dozen years.

Such people who survive or still keep coming have a sense of anachronism in the true sense of the word – of being against the hour, out of time. The new brutalism, in politics as much as in architecture, has superseded them. They exist but on sufferance, Girondins obliged to accommodate the Mountain. They are elected to the Shadow Cabinet because they have talent and because a majority favourable to such people and to talent itself still survives in the Parliamentary Party. Giles Radice, who looks immensely like Charles James Fox, is indeed an old Whig, a Fabian, a former research officer of that beautiful and ineffectual engine of union moderation, the General and Municipal Workers' Union. Quite what is going on is a doubtful question. But it is a source of dissatisfaction to all concerned. To what end has the Left spent all these years confecting its power and getting purchase on the election of the Leader, if major offices are still being satisfactorily discharged by the likes of Cunningham and Radice (who by reason of the General and Municipal connection are practically brothers-in-law)? But what shall it serve a man to gain the Shadow Department of the Environment if the party as a whole has by gradual crab-like *agiornamento* shifted far to the Left, and if the reselection process waits like a thief in the night in a paragraph somewhat weighed down by biblical metaphors.

In practice Neil Kinnock, a shrewder man in intention than in execution, is almost certainly happy with a state of affairs that preserves the maximum degree of up-front normality. He understands quite well that Labour needs all the acceptable faces it can lay its hands on. He has a low urge, which would shock Mrs Thatcher, to occupy No. 10 Downing Street. He actively dislikes all the nastier manifestation of the far Left. The beneficiary of Mr Jon Lansman's and Mr Vladimir Derer's reorganization of the Party's Constitution, he is a remarkably unrevolutionary chap. Whatever his blunders as a long-winded public speaker he almost certainly understands that a very left-wing Labour Party is a Labour Party very unlikely to be elected. And, sincere support for CND apart, he is, when left to himself, startlingly flexible on policy, as his shift on Europe indicates. He may have dithered, as a Labour Leader might be expected to dither, during the miners' strike, but his private loathing, well known to friendly journalists, for Mr Scargill, speaks for itself. The deal between the Soft Left, embodied not only in himself but in such pleasant men as Stanley Orme, and the old Right is agreeable to him. At a guess it is more agreeable to Neil Kinnock than to advisers like Robin Cook or Patricia Hewitt (or perhaps to Glenys Kinnock). He is part of old politics, content to have benefited from the changes but not otherwise welcoming them. An electable Labour Government depends upon such *Realpolitik*.

Yet the change is there. The reselection process functions and will run a few more heads into the guillotine yet. Accordingly, reassuring faces, solid men from the G. & M., amount to substantially less than they seem to. For the entire Parliamentary Party, the one assembly of moderate men, knows the route to the scaffold and behaves accordingly. Normality is a façade, a state of reassurance built up for the benefit not only of the electors but of the Shadow Cabinet itself. There is an understanding of the Party's crisis, which was not disguised by the brief friendly spurt in the polls. Nineteen-eighty, which was a conference of horrors, has gone away, but it can easily come back in 1987 or 1990, and meantime the reselection process will be piling Corbyn upon Clay, Michie upon Banks, the Hon. Pelion upon Ossa MP.

Giles is charming; Jack is brilliant. Both represent good and attractive strands of the Labour Party, which people have been leaving steadily for fifteen years. Their actual performance and that of their colleagues – more impressive to me than the legal sherpas upon whom Mrs Thatcher relies – is slightly tubercular, a last efflorescence in a patient whose bed chart has things upon it which it would be better for him not to see.

6

The Palace Guard

To say we get the government we deserve sounds downright defeatist. There is, however, a tendency to see the Government of Mrs Thatcher as a species of punishment, overdue but thoroughly deserved. Her popularity, which is periodically shored up with helpful disasters – the Falklands War, assassination attempts and the Labour Party – is of the sort enjoyed by school prefects of the harsher sort, and the god Kali. We have got ourselves into this mess; retribution in middle-aged female form is what we have coming to us. Life is not made any easier by Mrs Thatcher's visible enjoyment of the role. One of the great solaces of contemporary life would be a touch of relaxation or amiability or indeed silence on her part. It is alleged that two American senators made a call to Downing Street and that fifty-five minutes out of a possible sixty were given over to a lecture at the poor men. She is a reflex pedant tediously and unengagingly given to correcting Cabinet colleagues on irrelevant details from a treasure house of small-change information. Her sense of humour is a little above zero; as a speaker on public occasions she can be plain distressing, unsubtle, unrelaxed and a triumphant trumpeting scold.

The trouble with the present Government and its general tone is not that policies undertaken are wrong – they probably represent as intelligent a stab as possible at getting right the weakest economy in Western Europe – but that they are undertaken in a coarse-grained intolerant way. That is partly the result of their being different policies from the preceding consensus. The fool's paradise of reflation, statutory wage controls and open-ended public spending at which Mrs Thatcher rails was the easy resort of good-humoured, popular and relaxed politicians. Any fool, she would reason, can be affable on borrowed money, exactly describing the condition of President Reagan. But so great is the attraction of soft options and of things going on in the customary way that it takes a good deal of abrasiveness to fight your way out of it. At least it has always been true of Mrs Thatcher that while she may have the body of a weak and feeble woman, she has the broad personality characteristics of Smokin' Joe Frazier.

That however, is only the part of it. Abrasion is not co-terminous with aggression. Mrs Thatcher is very notable for lacking that aggressive instinct for a forward policy which is widely credited to her by admiring enemies. One close personal friend said to her face, 'I call you Cautious Margaret Cautious, Cautious Hilda Cautious Thatcher Cautious.'

Her visible triumphs – the switch of budget policy to heavy necessary cuts in 1981 and the Falklands War (if you think that a triumph) were achieved respectively through intense lobbying by the circle of advisers and civil servants closest to her and the blind besotted rage of the House of Commons. She took a long time to carve her enemies, leaving out-and-out conveyors of hostile report to the press, like Sir Ian Gilmour, where he stood for twenty-eight rather flap-handed months. 'Her first Cabinet was full of ill-wishers and even at the time of writing she carries with her the dismal ballast of Peter Walker, an outstandingly shallow, frequently wrong and sadly expensive Minister of the Crown (steel, milk, local government), who has gravely mishandled the Government's side of the pit dispute. Mrs Thatcher is neither as hard nor as decisive as she seems and likes to assert. To a gloomy degree she combines hard image with malleable substance, striking poses of the sort that would adorn Soviet poster art, yet functioning as Mrs Circumspect back at the office.

Having said all this and had oneself struck off invitation lists for twenty years, it is also necessary to concede that a genuine core of defiance and courage truly exists. The IRA did after all decide to murder Mrs Thatcher because she declined to give in to the excremental protest of the hunger and "dirty" strikes of IRA prisoners, refusing, absolutely impeccably, to give them political status. When one contemplates the long catalogue of weaseling acquiescence with which the British have broadly met protest providing it was outrageous enough, she did admirably. Specifically this Prime Minister is good when the pressure is on. All instinct is for caution and for conventional response, but thrust a spear to her throat and she becomes better than anyone could imagine. To digress hardly at all, the Thatcher–Howe–Lawson economic policy hurts terribly but, unlike the Reagan–Regan expansionist policy, it takes its pain now instead of deferring it to another date by the low expediency of borrowing money. They may not have very much imagination but they have not subjected the full effect of that policy to the false flush of interim borrowing. They will be proved right and it took a special quality of entrenched stubborn courage to stand fast. She does best when she trusts herself, does worst when older, wiser and more defeatist heads, early in a given conflict, persuade her to do the conventional thing.

The coal strike was such a long agony because the conventional wisdom, articulated by Mr Walker, feared to use the new union legislation and withheld the heavy artillery of rolling civil damages at half a million a time. These, given the broad rapacity of the NUM leadership, would have been persuasive. Walker was afraid of decisive action and built his own fantasy world of an early return to work, fed by audible chatter about the extent of coal stocks. Such flinching, boasting and non-performing frightened Arthur Scargill like a cotton-wool hand grenade. With all of this, Mrs Thatcher, trying to be wise, went sadly along, though fair-minded sources insist that she favoured early legal action but was dissuaded. She is conscious that a large body of solemn, self-important opinion shakes its head at every decisive, strong or radical act and awaits a return to the normality of graceful overspending. The spirit of social defeatism has sunk into some commentators like gin into a vagrant. Their expectations, like the very similar political geology of back-bench and civil-service opinion, make her tarry. In particular they make her concentrate on that limited section of the front where she can make some progress. The rough general purpose of this Government is to reduce public expenditure in order to make possible cuts in real taxation for productive purposes. The aforementioned gin and geology of received standard opinion make all such efforts desperately difficult. Very high interest rates, although not exactly seen that way, were a softer option in the early days than a considered, thought-out plan of reduced public expenditure. At the end of the road there is the frustration of being circumscribed, of very high unemployment and expenditure, which grows merely to cope with that unemployment. It is partly for such reasons that the Prime Minister's *manner* makes up for unaccomplished policy. Mrs Thatcher has been singing in part as a *Heldentenor*. She is bidden to relax but the emery paper in her manner is its own tribute to the accumulated frustrations of office.

She is, remember, leading a political party historically devoted to the occupation of office for its own sweet, hollow and echoing self. Historically the Tories have been devoted to the moral equivalent of the ministerial limousine. They forgive Mrs Thatcher her serious purpose only because she has miraculously managed to combine it with an unprecedented piece of the electoral equity. Mr Norris McWhirter of *The Guinness Book of Records* informs us that on 2 January 1988, before statute requires a new Election, Mrs Thatcher will have been Prime Minister for the longest continuous period this century. It is the least important thing about her but the main reason why her Party, bred in fecklessness and perfectly constituted for micro-economics and champagne, submits in astonishment to as much tight money and Horatio Algerian rhetoric as it does. Even so a serious-minded Conservative Party, like a reformed papacy, is always a tentative proposition. Ironically, political success has marched arm in arm with an economic policy virtuous but not yet rewarded. Investment has gone admirably up, but the unemployment figures have limped grimly up beside it, courtesy of President Reagan, interest-rate hitcher to the universe. The currency, caught between the millstones of US interest rates and the proletarian authenticity of Arthur Scargill, has been ground like Costa Rican special blend. All that Mrs Thatcher and Nigel Lawson can do is tell the economic truth and sit out the reflex panic of the older and wiser heads. This crisis of nerves was supplemented in the late summer of 1984 by a plague of bishops, descended like crickets and making socially conscious noises – mostly by rubbing their back legs together.

The Prime Minister has one thing going for her. After her first term she was able to reshape her Administration. The overtly hostile (the chorus of backbiters) have gone – with the unwise exception of that extinct molehill, Peter Walker. Walker, despite the bondwasher's baroque of his speaking style, is still able to proclaim non-existent genius to the winds. For the rest, Mr St John-Stevas long ago disappeared into a museum of outmoded chic, and Sir Ian Gilmour occasionally reads rented epigrams out of the corner of his mouth. Mr Francis Pym somewhat vengefully sought out and sabred down while the breath of the returning officers still hung in the air, 'Francis, I need a new Foreign Secretary', wrote a rather stylish book in temperate praise of the temperate. He is not a nasty man, though one excessively serpentine in simple matters. In *The Senate of Lilliput* he appears saying, 'People are not happy,' and now provides a welcome stretch of continuity in a changing landscape. They still aren't happy. They form 'Centre Forward'.

But what a change there has been. The Capability Brown aspect of Mrs Thatcher's personality has applied itself to little hills and stretches of plain, though no discernible folly, unless Viscount Whitelaw so classifies, is to be seen. Labour may have rearranged its Shadows, the Prime Minister has resculpted the ministerial undulations. Quite the cleverest move was to fill 'the great offices of state' with people either so new or so durable that early removal is not in prospect.

Having done five years at the Treasury, Geoffrey Howe transferred to the Foreign Office where, with the *Sitzfleisch* of mistaken matrimonial ambition, he seems likely to stay quite as long. Though if Mrs Thatcher had been a true radical or had possessed the fierce nerve to do it, the Foreign Office, with its superfluous energy and economics sections and its built-in philosophy of orderly retreat, might constructively have been demoted to the level of a simple Ministry on approximate par with Agriculture. A Ministry of Overseas and Consular Services is appropriate to our condition and to the Foreign Office's performance. However, since Geoffrey Howe declines to go to the Lords, he must be furnished with its departmental equivalent.

The equivalent moves of Nigel Lawson and Leon Brittan into the Treasury and the Home Office may serve on a modest scale to help us follow the wise practice of the Soviet Union where the excitement has been taken out of reshuffles by Ministers of Transport staying in post for thirty-nine years. Both men are close to Mrs Thatcher; both quite young if any politician ever is; neither is going anywhere else. Lawson has, and Brittan like a good barrister is rapidly acquiring, technical expertise. This will be fathomlessly tedious to the mass of us, but in the head of a big department is actually quite useful. With luck Brittan could be on his third reorganization of the probation service ten years from now. It will keep him out of trouble, and, given the low quality of Home Office civil servants, may actually lead to a full-scale reform of that department. The fashionable phrase is 'learning curve', but a serious man in a bad Ministry could more profitably start a slow pilgrimage by which he learns all the shrines at which his officials pray and which cow bones they treasure as relics. In time a Minister so informed may institute his own enlightenment; well, we can dream!

Lawson, a former City editor, who has been in the Commons only since 1974, is surely equipped for precisely the job he has. In getting value out of Lawson you must make a conscious jump from the public profile to the private intelligence. Publicly Nigel Lawson is a counter-productive man. Good-looking, but stoutish and thick-jowled, he looks like the Prince Regent on a diet. Indeed a high stock, open high collar and royal-blue swallowtail coat would suit him better than any drab clothing of the late twentieth century. He has the sort of ineradicable arrogance of an intellectually consistent, honest and rational man. There is almost no simulation or window dressing of any kind. For my money (and come to think of it, my money it is) Lawson is precisely the sort of Chancellor of the Exchequer we should have. He is just about as little of a politician as it is possible for a politician to be. As a public speaker he has most of the qualities of corrugated cardboard. Words worry and confuse him; at numbers his mind darts out like a lizard's tongue. Stumbling blindly in ill-articulated argument with the Deputy National Inquisitor, Brian Walden, he heard his tormentor say that our unemployment was much higher than in Europe. 'No, it's not,' he came back in the first sharp moment of a dismal performance. 'We have 13 per cent. Their average is 11.' It wasn't a vital moment but all conjunctions with figures are impressive; all attempts to find words swallow him up. Not surprisingly his very first Budget speech was one of the best on record by reason of being so little of a speech – he was wonderfully terse – and so much of a balance sheet. This may account for the degree of sympathy between him and the Prime Minister. As a speaker she can cope but she also has a mind that exalts and is preoccupied with figures.

Lawson is thus an entirely functional Chancellor. No one has dressed the stone or pointed the mortar. He exists to take the wind when it blows and not to fall down. Despite the Regency look, nothing about Heartless Nigel is for decoration. That very epithet is an unlucky product of his infelicity and intellectual integrity. For on the spectrum of political sympathies Lawson should be counted among humanitarians and liberals, as Mrs Thatcher, with her taste for naval battles and executions, should not. To make a point which reluctantly has to be repeated, he is bone dry but not remotely right-wing. He is, in short, a natural for the Treasury with its rigour of mind, passion for high intelligence and general superiority to all other Departments of State. He is also a perfect suicide pilot.

The necessary things will be done according to his intellectual convictions (and it is interesting how the word 'intellectual' either as adjective or noun recurs in the context of Lawson) with very little regard to pleasing either other politicians or the general public. He is a mechanism for rational action, almost a protected species in politics.

He is also, in the words of another member of the Cabinet, 'the single most original mind in government and the most fertile source of creative ideas'. Even from the Gallery, where we see his weakest and public side exposed, some idea of his quality is discernible. If he fails, he will fail absolutely and the Government with him, unless he is aborted first in favour of some slighter, more pleasing talent. But should he succeed, there are no political rewards. He is an unthinkable candidate for the prime ministership; as for other jobs, he would be no good at them and they no good to him. We have a formidable, principled mind at the Treasury, temperamentally indisposed to panic (despite the panics thrust upon him), fascinated by the problems, tempted in no way to advance himself by tinfoil solutions that start up cries of 'Good old Nigel'. Despite the agonies of sterling, we have put our collective shirt on consistency.

Leon Brittan may harbour higher ambitions, but he would be unwise to encourage them. One of those examination-passing, prize-taking, one-dimensional people not entirely unassociated with the University of Cambridge, he also speaks to the world, outside a small circle of friends and the very clever, with great difficulty. But while Lawson actually gives the impression of not envying the talents he lacks and of finding public debate a constitutional chore, Brittan makes the effort. He is a protégé of Willie Whitelaw, honourably determined to promote gifted people remote from his own social niche. He has been the object of some malice, and his candidacy in Richmond in the North Riding was vigorously opposed; Trollope would have disliked him intensely. He lacks grace and natural human sympathy, not finding it easy to communicate or perhaps to feel warm sentiments. In his Department, his intelligence, however lonely it must be in that stretch of departmental outback, can only be helpful. The rational thing is to keep him in the job for a sustained period (though he may entertain notions of being a rather more flexible Chancellor). It is equally important, despite one or two goodish performances in the House and at Conference, to disillusion him of the idea that he is a natural political leader. He is a highly intelligent subordinate, the sort of well-regarded sherpa who may well be included in the mountain-top photos should the party ever get there; but in no wise will he be put in charge of an expedition. Life as a henchman can be very rewarding as long as you settle for it. Conceivably he might hope, in a well-ordered market, to command the Great Seal in a few years' time when the interminable and unterminated Lord Hailsham's successor has seen out *his* term. But essentially Brittan has been promoted beyond his years in order, like Lawson, to perform.

The secondary effect of putting Lawson and Brittan in charge of cash flow and dungeons is to grind other aspirants into the dust and lower their sights. It is all rather like monetarism, the less you have of a given delight to hand round, the more you value it. Men who dreamt of higher things would now feel grateful for a piece of the DHSS. Mrs Thatcher is like a child rationing out licks of her lollipop, awarding them only to very nice, well-behaved children.

However, the principle behind her dealings with Mr Heseltine has been to preoccupy him with a ministerial gobstopper. The Department of Defence, weighed down as it is with admirals and ladies for peace in woolly jumpers, has the great virtue of swallowing up Mr Heseltine's vivid and somewhat primitive emotions like blotting paper. Heseltine is actually a good manager who deserves occupation and business. He has welded the Chiefs to Staff together like three elderly codgers doomed to share the same shelter on the promenade. He has helped see off the dreadful women of Greenham Common, those camp followers with a difference; and indeed their spiritual leader, Monsignor Bruce Kent, has acknowledged a major defeat for the Inadvertent Friends of Soviet Strategy by withdrawing from the chairmanship of a peace movement not discernibly moving at all. At the same time, the Minister of Defence we see at Party Conferences, who in the prior black exile of Environment had manifested himself without the encouragement of a full moon – mace-twirling, hundred-miles-per-hour, Prime-Minister-denouncing Heseltine – has been put wisely aside. It is rather as if Dr Jekyll, preoccupied with a busy and meritorious medical practice in Portsmouth, had stuffed Hyde into a strait-waistcoat and put him under sedation. The new Heseltine, like the new Nixon, requires to be looked over periodically but, again like Nixon, he is a useful fellow. Poor Julian Critchley, who functioned as Court Correspondent, a sort of Audrey Russell to the coming man of internal Opposition, has been left without an occupation. Heseltine, preoccupied with a major Department, has not lost his ambition but he has put aside childish things.

His promotion, according to some sources, was the inspired idea of Cecil Parkinson, who respects his ability and wanted it applied to something more useful than borough councils and smouldering resentment. Parkinson himself, a victim of *The Times*'s new prurience and one of the nastiest outbursts of private spite and public sanctimony one hopes ever to see, is very badly missed, so much so that a return in some office must be in serious prospect. Clearly, Mr Parkinson will return before the end of 1985, perhaps as Trade Secretary again in a swap with

Norman Tebbit whose short-term destiny must be to fill the empty chair occupied by Selwyn Gummer. For the Conservatives as a party, though they are more professional, more generally competent and even still – I speak rashly – rather nicer than they used to be, lack 'communication skills', a phrase to be printed only in cast-iron inverted commas. They can't explain themselves without seeming either apologetic or pompous. They are vulnerable to the first facile and plausible debator to take them on. The triumph of Mr Ken Livingstone – in the teeth of the things Mr Livingstone has actually been doing – eloquently demonstrates the problem. Parkinson, who has a nice way of talking quietly to camera, of not getting huffy or reciting the departmental brief like a prayer for the dead, was incomparably the best Chairman the Tories have had in recent times. The unwritten regulation that prefers chastity to competence bears very heavily upon them.

Mr Gummer, Chairman too long for health, has had too many unkind things said about him. Despite his good conduct after the horrors of the Brighton bomb, he does exemplify the life politician who takes seriously and speaks seriously about those matters which we find less throbbingly urgent than the Australian football results. The most important thing a Party Chairman has to do is not to reorganize Central Office, a place where the really dirty politics of Westminster take place, but to go on TV and face the entire Shadow Cabinet seriatim. Prime Ministers retain their value, in the manner of royalty, by keeping the Presence on short supply. Like turkey they should ideally be a once-a-year treat. The Chairman by contrast is a working mouth. Crews of nine cameramen doing the work of three should at every television studio in the country grow as familiar with him as with Sir Robin. Endearing and decent though Gummer is, it seems inherently unwise to identify the Conservative Party nationwide with an evangelical wolfcub. Gummer for Minister of Transport! Nicholas Ridley, that snappishly *fainéant* reconstruction, having been reduced to the condition of hamburger steak by the displeasure of Lord King, the opening looks ready made.

Otherwise, however, the Government looks all too solid. The sorts of talents that can cope with small oceans of departmental paper tend themselves to become rather superior bureaucrats.

The question is how do we distinguish the Samson figure, the blind drudge 'Eyeless in Gaza, at the mill with slaves' (on an incremental scale with their own pension scheme), from the Minister who can elevate drudgery into indispensability. This Godolphin character, to attempt a daring leap of metaphor, is never in the way, never out of the way and to him greater things will accrue. The feeling is, as Whitehall would express it, that Norman Fowler, who swims in the DHSS without troubling the lifeguards, is best placed to make this particular move. He has patrons and no very vigorous enemies. He is working hard to invest passion in a pedantic manner; he still grips the despatch box like a sprinter's block and he still drives sketch writers to quiet desperation by a spectacular ordinariness unspoilt by the little slips or incoherencies that constitute good copy. (The day will come when one of us is going to slip sugar into Mr Fowler's petrol.) Even so I would put money on him as a future Minister of Trade and Industry. He has an optimum combination of high competence and political neutrality, and he is as controversial as watercress.

Controversy itself is not quite what it was. Sectarian fires have not actually gone out but they flicker quite low compared with the days when Sir Ian Gilmour was doing his Malvolio exit: 'I'll be reveng'd on the whole pack of you!' – a point where eager young men now in the Queen's service were confiding, quite truthfully, that 'she' would be spared no mercy if the Party lost. The Tories have suppressed the sort of hatred that cannot be ignored among American Republicans, for whom East Coast patricians and the Jack Kemp–Newton Gingrich Radical Right element are irreconcilable constituents of the same Party. The British Tories were displaying until lately what could pass in a poor light for good nature. Success, while it lasted, spoilt them. If you want real street violence go to the Conservative clubs in the universities where your credentials are checked at the door and where an old time Labour Party effect can be had by speaking ill or well of certain Ministers. A man of peace, I always confine myself at such gatherings to discussing Norman Fowler.

Long the symbol of diminished abrasiveness was Sir Keith Joseph. Almost no Minister has been subject to so much ignorant and offensive vilification. No one has been so often prophesied for deletion. This stems partly from a vein of gentle eccentricity, natural in a don which is what Keith Joseph is, partly from the built-in antipathy of so many correspondents to the free-market ideas that he has rationally and bravely argued for. The revulsion with which a new idea is greeted among politicians and journalists is of an almost religious kind. Accustomed, like the Chinese, to sweep ancestral graves on appointed days, they expect fixed and recurring returns to incomes policies and conciliated pay settlements. Inevitably they took to Joseph as to a notably mild but intolerably persistent missionary. Despite the brief dreadful episode of university grants, when he touched upon the privileges of the middle class to enjoy state transfer payments, his reputation has steadily recovered. Perhaps the state of education in England after twenty years of free-range enlightenment has quietly shocked even the Tory establishment. Their record, like Mrs Thatcher's own, in the sector to which *their* children do not go, is unforgivable.

With housing premiums in the laagers of selective education steadily mounting, with the private sector taking more than it can carry, with a general acknowledgement that illiteracy and innumeracy are the growth points of the economy, a Minister of Education able to sort out ideas becomes popular. Joseph's rigour and seriousness began to be appreciated by those who had derided him. At the same time a notion of the man's moral stature, his decency and grave goodness began to dawn all round. Surprising things are said these days about Sir Keith within the civilized part of the Labour Party. Bearing in mind the civilized slaughter of grammar schools by Anthony Crosland out of God knows what fit of social vengeance, this is small enough amends. If, within the system, it is tacitly conceded that education desperately requires a return to first principles and utility (as most violently distinguished from social relevance), it is fascinating to find the political world in general agreement that Sir Keith is going about it in roughly the right way. However, courage on teachers' pay has not helped him.

Let us consider Mr Peter Walker. Fairness demands that this Minister's command and self-confidence should be marked to his credit in a Party noted in debate for self-doubt. Mr Walker does not offend, indeed there is a touch of solo trombone in most of his performances. He understands and plays the press like a pipe whose stops he knows. Not only is his former research assistant, Andrew Neil, a devoted roller of logs from the editorial office of the new *Sunday Times*, but the politically unsophisticated Sir Albert Lamb, the most recent editor of the *Daily Express*, is convinced that he is Peter's favourite journalist. But the truly exciting and innovative aspect of Mr Walker is his ability to combine brilliant success as a politician – a runner for the succession, everywhere spoken of respectfully, the notes of the pipe playing a sweet and caressing tune – with sustained and substantial failure as a departmental Minister. At Industry he encouraged the expansion of iron and steel on the very eve of iron and steel's collapse. At Agriculture he announced to dairy farmers what he elegantly and originally called a 'bonanza'. Hardly was the next reshuffle complete and Mr Walker secure at the Department of Energy than the distress slaughter of dairy cattle began.

A Minister who functions so extensively as a news agency reporting his own very wonderful achievements should remember that his ministerial career is an archive. He is also fortunate in the subordinate or subsequent errors of others. Mr Jenkin handles the abolition of the GLC and the metropolitan authorities like a man conducting an open-ended dialogue with the Eumenides. Yet it was Peter Walker who actually created the metropolitan counties, giving them fee-ed full-time councillors and setting them enthusiastically on a course of high (and inflationary) spending that it took a Labour Government to curb and restrain.

Mr Walker is indeed, as correspondents and editors fresh from their flattering briefings proclaim, a superb politician. As a Minister of the Crown he sometimes seems to have cost us about half a million a day over ten years. His good fortune continued in the person of Mr Ian MacGregor. The head of the NCB conducted affairs with the aplomb of an elephant trapped on the top floor of a department store, so all blame duly fell on Mr MacGregor. But it was the Secretary of Energy who had planned a strategy based on an early return for work, something that in the fiftieth week looked ill-advised. It was Mr Walker who strenuously opposed early use of civil legal action against the NUM, arguing that it would stop the early return he expected and bring Nottinghamshire out. The path of victory was specifically warned against by the Secretary for Energy. And the mistakes made by the Coal Board, while inexcusable, were precisely the sort of despairing actions that are made after many months of not getting precisely that promised early return.

The personality of Peter Walker remains what it has always been – marshmallow sprinkled with iron-filings – a man of quite awesome conceit who, to resume our stock-market metaphor, earnestly pushes his own shares, but whose verifiable assets have a wobbly and mystical appearance. His luck may make the Prime Minister's good fortune look like a talent for finding halfpennies, but man cannot live for ever by a combination of public-address system and serendipity. Walkers are a high-quotation, high-risk stock and not for institutional investors. He puts one in mind of Lord Chesterfield's definition of sex (not that he is so good as that): the price is exorbitant, the pleasure transient and the position ridiculous.

The Scottish Secretary, George Younger, is a politician sometimes tipped for advancement, whom nobody much dislikes. He counts as a wet but argues that Scotland, with its best middle-class talents in their third century of flight, is divided between unemployed Clydeside council tenants and unspeakable deer-shooting gentlefolk, so that redistributive tendencies are inevitable. It is Mr Younger's special genius that he can get money out of the Prime Minister at the flick of a little finger. Cautious, cautious Hilda is by all accounts quite terrified of the re-emergence of Scottish Nationalism. Mr Younger is skilled at playing subtly upon those taut little private nerves to get the funds he thinks necessary after very short interviews. Such shrewdness suggests a man easily underestimated (but not very much). When one adds that, by dint of a little kicking and screaming, he succeeded in having the cup of Northern Ireland pass from him, some respect is in order.

The inherent minorness of certain Ministers is almost the guarantee of their continued survival. One does not look to Nicholas Ridley for merit, though as an Etonian Dry he has a certain collectability. His two terms in office – first as the pilot of Mr Heath's Industry Bill, a measure so corporatist that it should have made him turn in his desk, then as the adversary of Lord King over redistributing the air routes of British Airways – have

111

not seen him to advantage. He responded to the British Caledonian lobby and its chief back-bench steward, Mr Robert McCrindle, by attempting to beat up Lord King's cherished collection of world routes at the very moment when British Airways had been transformed into a bundle of profit. As an enterprise it was the approximate equivalent of mugging Arnold Schwarzenegger. But Ridley, who is irretrievably dapper in thought as appearance, insisted in going gamely above his weight. Lord King has visited him in hospital. More creditably Ridley is the author of a memorandum written seven years ago advising the Government to take security measures against a siege strike run by, say, Arthur Scargill. Stressing the need for high coal stocks and heavy saturation policing, its early disclosure by some loyal civil servant produced the usual paranoid Assistant-Commissioners-under-the-bed flapdoodle to which we have become familiar. It was, on the whole, rather good advice – an attempt at contingency thinking to resist the next Saltley coke depot. No one should blame Nick Ridley for the failure of the Government to think *beyond* his proper and sensible proposals. There are people who want to turn this country into their own barbarous likeness; all steps taken to make this less likely will be called authoritarianism; that is the dialectic of the times.

A victim of another kind of dialectic has been Patrick Jenkin, whose time at Environment can surely not long continue. The world well knows the events of 1984 when the preliminary legislation for abolishing the GLC was defeated (for a year) in the Lords after strenuous lobbying by those two champions of decentralization, Mr Heath and Mr Rippon. The Minister actually deserves some sympathy. The Tories have been like a non-boiling pot on the topic of rate reform for longer than historical memory, and can't deliver. This frustration, together with the ostentatious agitprop and a disposition to spend money like the Trevi Fountain demonstrated by Mr Livingstone, drove the Conservatives (Mrs Thatcher rather than Mr Jenkin) into a furious desire for financial retribution. For once a soft line would have done wonders. Mr Livingstone's chief financial delinquency was to make heavy uneconomic cuts in transport fares. Left to himself he would have had hideous bills on his hands. A very uncontroversial little Bill putting a ceiling on the absolute contributions of the business rate could have had a furious public in the marginal GLC seats paying a directly attributable Livingstone rate and voting accordingly. Instead Mrs Thatcher, through the usual nod and wink channels, set a local borough and the Law Lords on to the GLC Chairman, thus making him into a martyr and getting him out of his expenditure troubles. It takes unwanted dexterity to nail a man on a cross and get him off the hook at the same time.

As for the GLC Abolition Bill (more precisely the Paving Bill), it was never going to be precisely popular, having just that touch of peremptory heavy-handedness that characterizes the Prime Minister fighting somebody smaller. But Jenkin anyway has all the wrong qualities for sustained controversy. He is a conscientious, truthful, rather literal-minded technician preoccupied with the mechanics of law and unable to make the political running. It was Jenkin's instinct to nominate a quango to fill the extra year. For that matter, he is unable to respond in the right tone of voice. A Jenkin speech is always something of a pilgrimage from firstly to lastly. Jenkin himself, lacking the virtue of aggression and the vice of self-protection at the expense of others, failed to do two things crucial to his own standing. He didn't counter-attack and he failed to call off-the-record press meetings to expand on his own unease. He was a clumsy but loyal Minister and he plodded, hands over neck, back hunched and knees bent, through the shrapnel. His failure indicates the limitations of Mrs Thatcher's passion for technicians. For Jenkin lacked no particle of serious fact about his Bill and brief. He knew them with the minute, oppressive detail of a good lawyer but we are in the Coliseum and you need gladiators. Patrick Jenkin is at heart a combination of scroll-keeper and High Temple functionary.

In the services of Ceres, goddess of grain, we have Michael Jopling, retired Chief Whip of the old-fashioned sort, friend and neighbour of Willie Whitelaw. A large, heavy-boned, worried-looking man without enemies or any especial distinction, Jopling is an inoffensive representative of the older, landed, unideological Tory. A rather straight-up-and-down man, without baroque ornamentation, he takes a lot of pains but has no notable flair for the House. Agriculture, a subject that could, in the light of the Old Spanish practices of the Common Market, be an area of furious controversy, is so far happily anaesthetized. Dullness in areas of extreme dubiety is no trivial virtue in the presiding Minister. And it should be said that Jopling, a life-long serious farmer, gives an impression of being less at ease than many with the rural-bureaucratic *omerta* that sustains overproduction for a market of 150 desperately needy cold-storage depots and converted RAF hangars; there is a likeability to the man. Any fire on the Thames he can be trusted to put out, but he is part of the soldiering-on tradition that gives the British Tory Party greater stability than its alternatives elsewhere. Such men are the genuine voice of the rural acreage and, unlike gentrified beer-baronets, they do not stamp out of politics in a temper saying that the Government in which they served is heading for the rocks. Michael Jopling has his failings but he deserves better than the inspired press campaign aimed at him.

Concerning Douglas Hurd, Secretary of State for Northern Ireland, I wrote in *The Senate of Lilliput* a number of unflattering things about his time at the FO, but also predicted the inevitability of his entry into the Cabinet – an instance of being right in all particulars! Hurd did nothing at the Home Office, to which he subsequently moved, to suggest that low opinions were otherwise than well founded. In Committee, where practical working relationships are struck up despite the long mornings of animus-by-numbers, and where you may hear spokesmen of Party X speak distressingly well of the man from Party Y, Hurd was not admired by opponents. He was allegedly underbriefed and by all accounts underattentive, regularly answering questions with a promise to write a letter, a fallback position which, like the use of a long-stop to a medium-pace bowler, says very little for the wicket keeper. He gave the impression of having brought the full feather-hatted grandeur of the Foreign Office with him to a despised secondary Department, and of regarding the Police and Criminal Evidence Bill (a thumpingly controversial piece of legislation) as better suited to his diligent Junior, David Mellor.

Hurd is one of those cold, unfriendly men about whom assiduous folk rush around assuring one that he is deeply warm and sympathetic. The analogy of Mr Edward Heath or of some deep-frozen mammoth is too close for peace of mind. In the

House he has the style and flair of one of those sacrificial, strangled corpses recovered from ten feet of Danish peat bog by Professor P. V. Glob. Come to think of it, do the Irish deserve any better than a warm and friendly Glob-corpse to preside over their affairs? The appointment itself had a ring of mutual despair about it. At 54, Hurd, an oversold commodity, was getting quietly desperate. The Prime Minister on the other hand had found that the departure of Mr Prior from that dismal job among the other bog people had created a vacuum which, far from being abhorred, seemed to be rather well thought of. If Northern Ireland is not to be governed by the equivalent of Captain Sleeman who put down thuggee with a platoon of Sepoys, then anybody can do the job. If contemporary politicians had to govern nineteenth-century India, they would instigate initiatives with spokesmen for the Thug community.

And who more satisfactorily meets the definition of 'anybody' than the Rt. Hon. Douglas Hurd MP? Proud, conceited, passionless, an apostle of an ancient department given over to national acquiescence and departmental rampart-holding, he is another item of melancholy predictability.

The Foreign Office itself of course is now in the familiar hands of Sir Geoffrey Howe, who is being praised in the usual highly orchestrated way for a deal over Hong Kong. It is universally described as 'brilliant', 'superb' and better value than a McDonald's cheeseburger, or, rather more guardedly, 'the best we could have got'. Beyond saying that the success of the deal turns upon at least four frail contingencies, one of which is the immortality of Mr Teng Hsiao-Ping, one cannot dwell at length in this essentially domestic context upon Far Eastern diplomacy beyond not believing a word of it. As far as the Commons is concerned however, Sir Geoffrey remains his old fibrous, unnourishing, good-for-you self. Unwisely encouraged to think in terms of the succession, which will not be his, he lingers semi-ceremonially, getting off aeroplanes, inspecting guards of honour and being carried up the Mall with some other footling Foreign Secretary in the fifth landau. It is not a man's job. After the Treasury, which, to adopt Dr Johnson's drinking metaphor, was like brandy – a drink for heroes – Sir Geoffrey is back on the watered claret of the diplomatic round and under orders from the unengaging Sir Percy Craddock, a snappish Jesuitical little man whose devious style of argument arouses many things but not confidence.

The pity with Geoffrey Howe is that he is another man intended, in an exalted sort of way, to execute other people's policy – that of Mrs Thatcher, of Professor Alan Walters or Sir Percy. To a lamentable degree he has become a political version of what civil servants are supposed to be – permanent and subordinate – a perpetual Minister endlessly available. Perhaps I am too unkind for he is a decent, likeable man and certainly indestructible; but it is terribly hard not to take note of Muriel Spark's Miss Jean Brodie and her remark about chrysanthemums: 'Such serviceable flowers,' she observed. Drooping only slightly, Sir Geoffrey has put himself in business as chief chrysanthemum to the Thatcher Court. Sir Geoffrey is rather like Whitsuntide, wholly incredible but fixed forever on the calendar.

Upon Lord Hailsham, Lord Chancellor, I shall not dwell, partly because he is in the Lords, partly in the hope that he will go away; and with Norman Tebbit, I shall deal elsewhere in this book. What remains to be said of Mrs Margaret Thatcher's second Government as reshuffled and reconstructed is of a collective nature. She is, as Prime Minister, liberated from contemptuous people who regarded her Government as a low bourgeois intermezzo. Lords Thorneycroft and Soames, who found her absurd, find themselves under asphalt; Sir Ian Gilmour has joined his research assistant's footnotes; and Mr Stevas has been transformed into a Tyrolese wayside virgin, lamenting but firmly planted in the wilderness.

Accordingly, and after three years' delay, she is answerable for a Cabinet of her own choosing. It is rich in professional utilitarian men who can do a job either expertly, like Lawson, or through a fast study, like Brittan or Fowler. It does not make for excitement, but if we were to face another ten years of Conservative Government, as Labour Conferences clearly intend, this could cause a major unperceived change in politics. The long-stay Minister with no serious higher ambitions, who knows every trick of his Department, could, if the itch to shuffle were resisted, be a countervailing force against the Civil Service. That institution is neither good nor bad, simply at excessive advantage; permanently, as Stephen Potter would have said, one-up – indeed in a continuous, on-going, one-up situation. One of the hallmarks of the Haroldinuum, that barely interrupted period of thirteen years when we were misgoverned by the Earl of Stockton and Lord Wilson of Rievaulx, was of incessant departmental change (nine Ministers of Defence under the post-war Tories). Government is not a traffic intersection; men holding a post for fifteen months are unlikely to be much good at it. Departments themselves fall into demoralized apathy when they are everywhere perceived as stepping stones upon which the ambitious man may condescend to adjourn his career before proceeding to serious things. (Ulster has hardly benefited from being used by Mrs Thatcher at her most frivolous as a sort of punishment cell.)

Mrs Thatcher's liking for technicians may make the House of Commons a dismal place. It may increase the superiority complex of Labour Shadows who can perform more triple salkos than Ministers who, on the glazed surface of rhetoric and riposte, are sometimes no more sure-footed than Mr Winkle on the ice at Dingley Dell. But the impression that this Government increasingly presents to the world, as Saatchism bites ever deeper, is of a group of synchronized swimmers. Those who can bear to remember the Los Angeles Olympic Games will recall that synchronized swimmers move upside down underwater, for a period injurious to health, while keeping on their faces a sustained smile too imbecile for the marketing of face cream.

Mrs Thatcher is however an excessively serious lady. If she could divide politics exactly between doing and seeming, between the decorative and useful parts of government, she would buy the best façade on the market and concentrate her mind on the engine room. (With the Saatchis and Gordon Reece perhaps she does.) The trouble is that the British political system requires rough, inarticulate, boiler room artisans of the intellect – men like Nigel Lawson – to come on deck and, twisting their homely workmen's caps in their hands, give a credible account of themselves.

However poorly the Government may perform in the Commons (and too much is demanded of Mr Tebbit, Mr Biffen and the Prime Minister herself), it is now set into a pattern roughly of Mrs Thatcher's choosing, conscientious, hardworking, slightly peremptory but heavily legalistic. It is an alliance of old-style sceptics drawn from the great office-desiring reservoir of the most professional political party in Western Europe, hesitantly flecked with radical purpose. It is not an exclusive or doctrinally enclosed sect of a government. Doctrine and inter-party sectarianism are not quite the force they were, though everyone quietly measures everyone for his denominational tendencies. Certain essentials are taken care of and every effort is then taken to accommodate all strands of faith.

After their experiences at the hands of semi-automated clergy, 'Barbie Bishops', we might call them, the Tories may not care for this. But in James Callaghan's words, they are a Broad Church more troubled with schism than excommunication.

Three jobs require to be held for a political faction to rule – the chairmanship, the chief whip and the Treasury. The last is utterly secure; the first in the hands of an acknowledged underling; and the whips' office, despite Mr Wakeham's tragedy, is in friendly hands. Whatever it is Mrs Thatcher wants to build she now has men in all departments who will carry bricks for her. What more can the head of any reforming government ask? Failure or success now truly reside with her.

7

Imperatrix

In four to five years' time the first Countess of Kesteven, preceded by a herald in mothballed motley out of *Alice in Wonderland*, will take her seat in the House of Lords. Either she will have behind her something that can pass at forty paces for an economic recovery, or she will be the latest in a line of failures fled to ceremonial oblivion. Until then we are stuck with Margaret Thatcher.

That title, if she takes it, will derive from the part of Lincolnshire (long since fed into the gloppiter-gloppiter machine of local-authority redesignation) from which Margaret Roberts originally came. But then she has had a number of names – 'Snobby Roberts' for the sandblasted vowels of an ambitious provincial child learning in the immemorial awful English way 'to talk properly', and the 'Iron Maiden' to the Russians. To the far Left, who have a pleasing respect for her, she is 'Maggie, Maggie, Maggie – Out, Out, Out'. By my trepidatious colleagues in the Gallery she is called, rather nervously, 'The Lady'; the title which rather appeals to me is 'Baroness Belgrano'.

This Prime Minister, whatever her name, has managed to create an impression in Continental Europe – which, sadly, no serious-purposed British figure has done for thirty-five years. We are a diminished country and what has helped focus attention on our Prime Minister, even abroad, is the extent to which she acknowledged that fact and minded furiously about it. Her bitterest critic, her most derisively patronizing enemy

119

among the champagne-and-reflation Tories (with whom she has, after long provocation, dealt as Peter the Great with the *Streltsy*) would not deny her fervent concern to reverse that decline.

She is the inheritor of a string of evils that no economy could long bear. She took on the Jones–Aldington agreement between hard unionist and soft politician, which by enforcing statutory jobs at 'regulated' British ports has wiped them out; the poker-playing night shifts of British Leyland, which together with pitiful management made that company the toast of the German, Swedish and Japanese motor industries; a job-hoarding steel industry with nearly a fifth of its capacity concentrated on the open-hearth process invented in 1866. Although the unions can be rightly blamed for much of this, by no escape route will the British Tory Party, in its butterfly days, be excused. Britain had a chance to modernize and reform itself in the fifties. It chose instead to be governed by Harold Macmillan! The ultimate theatrical escapist now survives as the A. E. Matthews of politics where once he had been its Jack Hulbert. History will be harsher to Macmillan than to the Labour Government that succeeded him. Despite follies and misjudgements, Labour had a wider streak of probity than an Administration that ended with the 'dash for growth'. One would like to think that Mrs Thatcher is temperamentally the antithesis of the *fainéant* old charmer who, at his own urgent peremptory insistence, she made Earl of Stockton. But we shouldn't bank on it. The lady has a fair measure of theatricality and posture-striking in her own character, and we may yet in an evil hour look back at her as a sort of female Donald Wolfit.

In economic matters she can legitimately claim a degree of consistency if not success. Inflation is down and the power of the trades unions is satisfactorily diminished. It is at least the Government's principle to seek solvency. Even the Administration's untruths are touching. Unable to get the cuts and utility price increases it wanted, the Treasury, with Mrs Thatcher's blessing, chose to do some creative accounting and proclaim itself in a condition of Pickwickian credit when all who could count knew otherwise. This made it possible for Mrs Thatcher's Chancellor to claim that he had money available for tax cuts, which according to his rules he had not. We are still into the serious affectation of virtue, and it would not do for the Government to say that a billion's worth was going to be borrowed for sweeties. In Treasury matters renewable virginity is the least of the miracles on hand.

However, being fair to Mrs Thatcher (and to Mr Lawson who is in some sort *her* prime minister), there has been more rectitude than that episode implies. The hard lines over Steel, British Leyland and, indeed, over the coalfields have been right. One cannot see a single one of her Ministers, perhaps not even Mr Tebbit, quite going the full, hard, brutal distance that she has gone. When fools are through mocking him for clumsy public relations Mr Ian MacGregor will be appreciated for having put an American proposition to a British industry with the hard sense that implies.

A very high price was paid both to reform the coalfields and to meet head-on the physical-force trade unionism which has so charmed us lately. Every kind of mistake was made, especially by the concession-granting Department of Energy. Something very close to a Scargill victory was there for him to pick up in the early autumn had he been more flexible. Credit for winning belongs to the Prime Minister whose flair for vindictiveness was never put to better employment and who clearly recognized an identifiable sell-out when she saw one. Incidentally credit also belongs to the previous Secretary for Energy, Nigel Lawson, who had had the foresight to build up coal stocks. He takes so little trouble about his own profile that we must do it for him. But the singularity of purpose that does distinguish Mrs Thatcher from the generality of prime ministers, the ability to hang on and pay the price, is after all the reason for putting a very high value on her.

Scargill has been compared with all sorts of interesting people but 'King Arthur', also has affinities with George Hudson, the railway speculator of the nineteenth century who, by dint of optimism, over-quotation of assets and a bullying insolence that carried all the best judges of character with him, contrived to be known interestingly as 'King Hudson' or 'the Railway King'. In practice Hudson built not much over ninety miles of railway and contributed nothing to the economy except parody and a lesson about the unwise extension of credit. He was in due course exploded by patient, hard-bitten and unforgiving enemies.

It is too much to hope that Mr Scargill will, on this analogy, spend the next twenty years in frayed but sufficient exile in Boulogne, but one sees the charm of the idea. As for those who defeated him, they are perhaps inadvertent friends to the trade union movement for which Mr Scargill has long been a resident poltergeist. Mrs Thatcher, for all her bombast and vanity, has a touch of virtuous ruthlessness which makes the British feel very odd. In one sense they deplore it and long for some soothing, analgesic, wittering old love of a political teddy bear to make them feel comfortable. In another way they are delighted; softness is so nearly universally the norm among British politicians that the people are reconciled to defeat. Anyone who sees off Scargill, or for that matter refuses to concede anything to the Ulster IRA hunger strikers, comes as a sharp and gratifying taste on the political palate. Sheer difference, however much oversold, is half her secret.

And yet she can be so badly oversold. The episode of the Falklands War embodies all the endurance and fixity of cha-racter claimed for her; and, in low political terms, it was a comprehensive success, a hitting of the jackpot. But actually a good idea? A necessary war? A credit to us? That's quite another thing. We have all had time to digest the Falklands War and think about it, if such an aberrative course of action as thinking may be contemplated. It is, after the event, very hard to see the Prime Minister as controller or mastermind of anything in particular. Not for the first time, she looked entirely passive. The Foreign Office made its dreadful initial blunders, putting its hand on General Galtieri's knee under the negotiating table and screaming rape. The House of Commons divided between the irrational rage of the stupid Right (Julian Amery and his Orchestra) and the cynical but slightly over-calculating patriotism of the Opposition, anxious to loyalize the Prime Minister out of existence by supporting a military action they thought impossible.

Their intention was that a war should have been put into preparation that could not be won, probably not even fought. Either it would end ignominiously or be called off in the style of Suez: 'We have put out the forest fire.' Caught between the folly of her own side, the supersubtlety of the Opposition and her own fairly crude feelings, she gambled in despite of the missing air cover . . . and won. However, she appears to have been consulted minimally by the Navy at crucial moments. Indeed, the only explanation of the *Belgrano* episode that fits the evidence is that some senior naval person decided to commit a war crime. The Government was either tricked on inaccurate information into changing its own rules of war or was a knowing party to an act of gratuitous killing. Either way it was left to cover for the indefensible and to suffer the death of a thousand questions from Tam Dalyell. In return for that war the Government obtained a glorious victory, a Roman triumph down the Strand together with a few thousand acres of mud, ideal for the resettlement of petrol-bombing pickets and for very little else. For this sodden wilderness we have paid out, so far, at a rough computation, 9.5 billion pounds, 258 British lives and the lives also of about a thousand Argentinians. It is said that the war helped the Government win its Election; even electioneering has its limits. We are also told that victory over the wretched Argentinians has caused us, as a nation, to feel good. When we are a little older and have thought a little more, it will make us feel very bad.

There is no question however of what the war did to Mrs Thatcher; it turned her into Brer Rabbit newly emerged from the briar patch, or perhaps into Big Mammy Wham-Bang-Big-Money. She had not sought the war; probably she had played no very conspicuous part in controlling the war, but she was destined either for the blame or the credit and when credit came she can hardly be blamed for rejoicing. But that triumph also put her on to a high and diminished her judgement. For after her re-election, Mrs Thatcher could, on that June night, have clapped her hands and told Admiral Nelson's stone lions to take her down Whitehall. With the sort of majority you could use as collateral, she could have done almost anything. In fact she buttered the pavement by undertaking a series of inept, arrogant things with no utility in them, one of which *was* impossible. She wished, God knows why, to appoint Sir Humphrey Atkins, that secondhand Lepidus, as Speaker over the head of the Commons's preferred choice, Jack Weatherill. It took her own Chief Whip, John Wakeman, to remind her of constitutional practice, that the Speaker is not, in Nicholas Vachell Lindsay's phrase, 'a slave, an echo, a suit of clothes'.

She proceeded, against the advice of most of the Cabinet, to the extirpation of trade union representation at GCHQ. (Yet it was not the civil servants' union that had withheld transmission by that intelligence station of the message from the Argentine High Command to the *Belgrano* that it should sail away from the Exclusion Zone and return to port.) The union concerned was headed nationally by one of the most moderate figures in the TUC; there had been a modest, open-shop union without harm for forty years. Quite what possessed her to crush this glow-worm underfoot, who can say, but certainly her old sensible dithering had deserted her. 'Jump first, break a leg afterwards' seemed to have become the maxim. (The leg has been mended in the docile Appeal Courts by the voodoo logic – 'national security'!)

With the matter of the GLC one has spoken elsewhere, but again it was doctrinaire, and very doubtfully useful. In particular the attempt to kill the spare year of the GLC's elected term, whatever one's fears that Mr Livingstone might buy the Uffizi on the rates, looked, and was, peremptory and wrong.

Then there was the matter of *Regina. v. Ponting*. Ponting was a shocking, sneaky civil servant; not too difficult to guess who *Regina* was. The Solicitor-General, in best Pavlovian style, retreated to his office, pulled down the blinds and thought about national security. The Prime Minister was, of course, quite blameless. The subsequent trial, the use of in camera proceedings and a summing-up in the traditions of the King's Bench in 1640 did for Mrs Thatcher's democratic image what salmonella does to the stomach. Despite the admirable acquittal of Mr Ponting (and every Department of State should have one), the hubristic authoritarian style of the lady and her creatures was established for good.

Such rows are irrelevant to the real business in hand. She wants an economy and will do painful things to get it. The private virtues with which she is credited are real. She, like Harold Wilson, treats not very important people around her with particular consideration and kindness. Despite two operations for a detached retina she exhausts herself in a minute struggle with a job she pays the compliment of taking seriously. And it is a job that brings out despair in all who do it. Far from 'enjoying the papacy now we are Pope', she is working the papacy to the knuckle. She may have learnt tactical cynicism but she has not submitted to strategic cynicism. She will manoeuvre and trade to get the things she needs, but she has not abandoned government for office. Yet for all her energetic authoritarianism she is so often a puppet on the hand of circumstance. Her reforms are part of a policy shared across party and across Europe by those who govern: the Socialists, Signor Craxi, François Mitterrand, even Señor Gonzalez, are all into cost-cutting, deflationary, subsidy-cutting policies. If they are following her, she is following James Callaghan. If things go right, if the world revives sufficiently for our penny wisdom to take advantage of it, there will be great credit for 'Thatcherism'; if not, not and she will have built a palace of lath. We shall spend a long time waiting; so long, that the things she gets wrong, the distractions, the acts of foolish imperiousness, may seem like the reflection of a long, melancholy, perhaps thinly rewarded, way ahead.

She always seems to travel with the knowledge that she is vulnerable. In British politics, unlike those of the United States where the most exalted member of the Cabinet is a hireling or fireling, a hundred-dollars-a-night Secretary of State, every British Cabinet Minister carries in his knapsack the knife with which he may, if the occasion arises, stab the Prime Minister. And for all her victories, that option remains. Towards the end of 1984 there were critics on hand to murmur at her again, though not in the arrogant assured style of 1981. She had to endure the lachrymose combination of kitsch, reminiscence and fallacy favoured by the 90-year-old Harold MacMillan in the Lords – 'The miners are the best people in the world.' No, they're not. But it is Margaret Thatcher who is stuck with the laid-up treasure of thirty years of such self-anaesthetizing rhetoric while the police must cope with the best people in the world throwing steel bolts.

Despite the jarring style and the truculence (sometimes enjoyable, as when she picked up Wedgwood Benn by his lapels and threw him across the Chamber with details of his own pit closures) and those moments of proud, baying vulgarity when one fears that the brass has entered into her soul, she *is* serious. Mrs Thatcher is mentally engaged, and has the powers of concentration to sit through a long struggle without ennui or desire for a fatuous empty formula. But, being serious, she is also hated, the first Prime Minister since Robert Peel against whose life an attempt has been made.

During the period of the miners' strike many efforts were undertaken, notably by bishops, to indicate that what is called 'the very fibre of our society' was being assaulted equally by the Prime Minister and the leader of the Workers' Militia. The Grecian-urn mentality, this half-witted passion for false symmetry, will enable their spiritual lordships to get it wrong and go on getting it wrong. The offer that was made to the NUM was an option of a comfortable football-pools win for those taking redundancy, and the guarantee of a job, but not necessarily in the same place, for those who wished to stay. It was an offer that historical fear of the miners had done something to construct, but it was also the embodiment of generous, conciliatory regearing. To have given way further before the half-crazy violence of the pickets, which truly managed to make South Yorkshire under picket rule look less like a free country than Poland, would have been the ultimate achievement of those Conservatives who have lived by retreat and the surrender of other people's interests.

Probably she will not succeed in her main task. For all serious reform in Britain, the last country in Western Europe truly to take itself in hand, is Promethean. Every attempt at Treasury rectitude is a struggle between the two themes of *Tannhäuser*: the Venusberg Music, all quivering high erotic strings (temptation and its acceptance), and the Pilgrims' March, which is dull, dour, though, in Wagner at least, triumphant.

Margaret Roberts's tutor at Somerville, Janet Vaughan, spoke, not altogether admiringly, of her being, at 19, 'set in steel in her convictions'. Now in working practice she has shown herself capable of sinuous retreat and has been garlanded with circumspection. She glided out of a fight with the miners in 1981 for the very good reason that she expected to lose; but her character, a fascinating heather-mix of vindictiveness and prudence, bid her be ready for any future conflict in circumstances where she would win. It is an un-British and deplorable approach and the best claim she has on us.

8

Consuls

Every session, every Parliament, has its heroes, the men who will be talked about in future generations. I would not necessarily put all four selected for special notice here so certainly high. But they *are* dominating this Parliament without any of them being the Leader of a major party. I mean Norman Tebbit, David Owen (Leader of a minor party) Robin Cook and John Biffen.

Writing in 1981 in the *Sunday Telegraph* I suggested that Norman Tebbit, then a Minister of State, possessed the qualities to become the Iain Macleod of his generation, if on a different wing of his Party. I stand by that. Tebbit is an extraordinary man. His reputation was of course originally based upon ferocious intervention from the back benches. That is the least of his talents and to the extent that the old harshness crops up occasionally in debate, it now hinders him. But at the time and for a few years when the Tories were dreadfully demoralized, the ferocity came like brandy to the half-drowned. A back-bench sortie by Tebbit in the early seventies was like a dash of tabasco added to rabbit stew.

All this, however, is far behind and began to be *put* behind on the first occasion when the Parliamentary Under Secretary at Trade rose to speak at the dispatch box. His transformation in thirty months into the Secretary of State for Employment has been described. What astonishes now is the domination of that personality in the House. It is not just wit, though he is witty (and give or take the occasional regression, much more kindly so than he was); it is not just his capacity for mastering a case. For, despite some uninformed sniping, he has a firm grip of the vast Portuguese Empire of Trade and Industry. What distinguishes Norman Tebbit is an infectious, pomposity-dispelling personality; he has a refined intelligence, and lightness of touch informs the most serious issues.

The Irish bomb in Brighton, which killed five people, maimed others and reduced Tebbit's much-loved wife, Margaret, to a condition close to paraplegia, nearly lost him to politics, and may do so yet.

Ironically, the Brighton murders permitted the early-morning public to see a side of the Minister that his friends have long argued and urged but without success. They tend to say 'he is a nice man; never mind the cleverness and talent for polemics. There is more warmth and broad affection about him than is altogether usual in a politician.' The man who was seen nationwide being dug out of the rubble saying, 'Get off my feet, Fred' and who was reported replying to the question, 'Are you allergic to anything?' – 'Bombs' conveyed more of that impression than the best-intentioned narrative ever could.

Despite a short fuse and the odd lapse into the unnecessary bullying of people he is rather fond of, like Peter Shore, he *is* a good-humoured man. The demon images we all know – Dracula, and, since he bought a cottage in Devon, the Hound of the Baskervilles – but these are relevant only as allusions to the past or to the odd night out crunching orphan backbenchers. The idea that if Chancellor he would refresh himself during the Budget from a small decanter of blood is merely part of the time warp in press perception. His style in office has usually been quite gentle; he does not need to raise his voice. Yet he has an ability I have only ever seen once before (in Brian Walden, Parliament's great departed lost talent) to obtain immediate quiet and attention – in Tebbit's case, simply by folding his hands together over the despatch box. Disraeli, according to Lord Blake, used to obtain a similar effect by passing his handkerchief from one hand to the next, usually as the prelude to a joke. Tebbit's unconscious gesture says simply 'The next bit is quite interesting, do listen.' And they do. An ass of a failed politician, whose habit it is to insult people by way of getting their names wrong, remarked privately, 'Well, as for Mr *Tibbit*, we shall have to see whether he is really quite intelligent enough.' Since then the Austin-Rover case, which involved devastatingly effective use of Tebbit's Trade Union Act (strike ballots); the persuasive prospect of ballots on political levies; the brilliantly executed sale of Inmos, and finally his judgement *in April 1984* about the pit strike lasting at least until Christmas, all make that observation quite outstandingly fatuous.

A far more interesting criticism is that Tebbit is not all that dry. One middle-rank Minister observed that, however much they might hate each other (and they do, they do), Heseltine, Walker and Tebbit held pretty much the same opinions. This is excessive. But certainly he lacks the Treasury tic and is willing to spend public money – vast amounts in conjunction with Keith Joseph on BL – and quite right too. That was a cash-for-power swap, which wiped out the destructive part of a union and began the resurrection of a hopeless company. Now this is not the Treasury way. Together with a rational desire for sound money, some Treasury Ministers, especially when they engage in petty cuts – like the million taken from the BBC Overseas Service – seem concerned less with saving candle ends than with putting out candles. This pettifogging facet of Treasury thinking often suggests minds bandaged up Chinese-style since childhood. It does not appeal to Tebbit any more than the blind expansionism of the latterday Macmillans. One is terrified of calling a politician whom one likes a 'pragmatist'. Poor Harold Wilson, trapped between his great understanding and his desire for quick effects, has done for that word for ever. Let us just say that Tebbit is an empiricist; he has a great bump of common sense. The desert of the correct Treasury line, closing everything and anything, while remaining coolly dispassionate about injuring productive manufactures (of which the Treasury seems slightly to disapprove) is not to his taste.

Also, as an old airman, having flown planes long-distance for seventeen years, he is something of a sucker, well, an enthusiast, for all things aeronautical. This made him a friend of the European Airbus, widely derided by knowing columnists and now selling rather well. Given power, he would never use it theologically. The Public Spending Borrowing Requirement would indeed be used, but as a signpost not a wayside shrine.

He would approve Treasury strategy but grow exasperated with Treasury tactics. He has the unusual gift of seeing things in perspective. 'Does this move serve Britain's interests?' 'Is that cut actually useful or is it so much hopeful watering of the hairs on one's chest?'

On the other hand, if not doctrinally dry, he is quite right-wing on certain issues. He was always in favour of executing murderers and, having been brought painfully out of rubble that still covered the victims of murderers, he will hardly be less so. But in matters of law and order generally, while his instinct would be harder than many Tory MPs who have grown oddly benign, he is far too cautious to throw authority about capriciously.

Tebbit is one of those rare people who mature and learn all the time; what he said last year is of diminishing importance because he is ingesting and responding to too much new data. The 39-year-old backbencher was a highly intelligent bundle of RAF, upper-working, lower-middle-class prejudices. Most men would have stayed that way. The Minister by contrast has limitless appetite for the things his Department can teach him. He was always clever, but to lapse from English, he has subtled up, leaving opponents sawing the air and attacking the ghost of the day before yesterday.

Tebbit accumulates layers of understanding all the time; and Trade, with its window on to the most advanced technologies and its preoccupation with the real getting and spending side of life, is probably the most instructive Ministry for the most responsive Minister. At the moment he is fascinated by folding-screen communications. These, if finally achieved, will bring compositors, machine-minders and the newspaper managements now cringing before them, into a different universe – a suitable place for both. If this idea does jell, the money now being ruinously expended on installing the interim technology while paying the printers not to smash it will look even sillier than it does already. It is nice to have a Minister taking notice of ideas ten years ahead of those likely to be directly concerned with them.

It is an important aspect of the man that he came into politics so comparatively late. He is short of that damaging self-importance and preoccupation with trivial political salami-slicing which marks the man who decided on a Parliamentary career at 15, held all the junior offices, read PPE or its equivalent, and, if he took employment, did so as a bridging overture before the curtain went up on the set of an over-familiar pantomime.

He is free from the limitations of those who looked at President Kennedy in 1961 and have spent their time ever since trying to call up that delusive dead fashion. Tebbit is not imitating anyone, though he learned a few tricks as a boy from Iain Macleod. As a result of a correspondence with Macleod he decided, in the mid-sixties, to give politics a go. From him he learned the habit of attack, but, being his own man, he has been unlearning it, handling the Commons with ever greater mildness and ironic charity. He lacks the self-doubt; the jagged tooth of insecurity and nagging uncertainty are attenuated. If he were defeated for the leadership he would neither moan nor linger.

And the most likely alternative leaders are men he would not now wish to serve under. No haunting Healey, he would be off and away if someone he despised took control, and he does despise secondary bankers rather. With one fairly remote exception to whom I shall come, Tebbit is the only man I can imagine doing the job now performed by Mrs Thatcher. He is the one certain personality, the Prime Minister apart, who can actually impress himself on history. He is neither mean nor petty, though he has those reserves of occasional brutality in debate. He speaks the English language when most are declining into prose fishmeal. He pays us (and here I acknowledge a gallery prejudice) the compliment of exerting himself in the Chamber of the Commons, helping to keep classical parliamentary debate alive where others read the order of service appropriate for burial at sea.

Norman Tebbit is very grown up indeed. Long before the bomb at the Grand Hotel, he came clòse enough to death as a young pilot, to recall the look on death's face. His crash-landed plane caught fire in a cornfield; no release button worked and he escaped only by smashing a window not designed for smashing. Your old-fashioned soldier turned to politics would understand such things, but political life is, thank God, increasingly civilian, and not many merchant bankers have learned so much so quickly. Life being a bonus to him has surely contributed to the uncomfortable sharpness of Tebbit's perception. After Brighton nobody will know the effect of that horror, though it will, *inshallah*, be benign.

. It is a personal instinct, a trusting to my own private judgement, that Norman Tebbit, if he became Prime Minister, would be a humane influence. For all his sharp edges and sardonic style, he is tall enough to see further than most. I end with a point made above but in need of underlining: he is neither petty nor mean, though given to anger. He is good news.

The other obvious mover forward in most people's perception during the last eighteen months or so, and one who, like Tebbit, learns as he goes, is Dr David Owen. Most of the praise for Owen is now as stereotyped as the general damnation that he attracted as Jim Callaghan's Foreign Secretary. Those not fond of him tend to make behind-the-hand remarks about 'the new Nixon'. But those two clichés are hard to get away from. It was Owen's way at the FO to be rude, dismissive, peremptory and very hard to work for. It is difficult at a diplomatic party not to encounter someone, gin and tonic in hand, who will sigh deeply and tell you about how the Doctor turned him into roadmaker's hard core. Taxi drivers a year or two back – 'I 'ad that Dr Owen in my cab. 'Ee's not nice' – were much the same. It may be that medical students and ward sisters have even more sense of hierarchy than civil servants, and take orders unsympathetically given more gratefully. It may even be that the reputation of that gracefully inconsiderable man, Lord Carrington, may owe something to the smooth solace of working for someone relaxed, however ultimately he was to show himself effortlessly wrong. Owen, admired or detested, is a class study. He is the exemplar of the doing, functioning, working middle classes who have never learned to lean on things. Interestingly, like the pilot Tebbit, he did a real job – as a hospital doctor – before coming into politics. He has the natural nonconformist virtues and the Welsh Nonconformist background with the prolixity edited out.

He is at home in America, is married to an American and has a critical warmth for things American. He was arrogant in his unpopular days, but it was the arrogance of activity, not the snobbish lassitude of old boy murmuring to old boy. The vanity, symbolized by the busy comb and the masterful dismissal of what he despised, gave him the look of a Mills and Boon, ward-walking, young hero. And politics, which, despite Mrs Thatcher, is largely a male activity, does not contain many people who are aroused by Mills and Boon. Shudders of unidentifiable sensual delight did not go through the average Transport-and-General-sponsored MP at the sight of the young Doctor's finely sculpted profile. He thought quite other things, and the company director sitting opposite tended to agree with him.

Owen's new dominance as SDP leader and Owen's old arrogance are kissing cousins. He has learnt, indeed, to temper and reduce the arrogance. He is politer and gentler in his Chamber style but he has not stopped being sure he is right and, wonderfully in a Party that was everywhere accused of limpness, he is as emphatic as an ice-axe. He was hired as a sharp edge and has hardly stopped cutting. It is a remarkable measure of his achievement that part of the deal done with the Liberals in the winter of 1984 allowed for more joint appearances of the Alliance's two Leaders. Now, for all his exhaustion and temporary debility, David Steel is a formidable public figure collecting favourable polls the way African politicians collect honorary degrees, yet he actually finds it necessary to have his time allocation downstage written into the contract. Who would have predicted that the son-in-law's chum, the Godolphin Horn of politics, who 'only smirked and nodded', should have won so much authority on his own as the Leader of a Party seven-strong in the Commons?

The vindictiveness of Mrs Thatcher in first barring him from the Cenotaph, then on conceding admission, granting precedence to the Leader of the Official Ulster Unionists, is its own sour little garland. The leader of the tiny SDP should not *need* snubbing. But since Owen took over from the sick and badly slowed-down Roy Jenkins, he has used the small pieces of territory available skilfully. The hooligans,* beside whom the SDP still sit, may helpfully shout him down occasionally, but the feeling is hatred not derision; and he is a bad man to shout down, liable to get himself on television news fighting for the right to speak.

---

* I mean the Official Hooligans led by Dennis Skinner, not the Provisionals of the new intake.

Another thing about Owen, and distinctly a development, is the temperate and practical nature of his criticism. He has discovered a vein of reasonableness which worries the Tories. Take Defence: he fervently supports national nuclear defence including an independent deterrent, but would have given negotiations one last whirl before taking Cruise; Trident he finds too big for our international boots and cripplingly expensive. He is almost certainly right and one looks forward in hope to the cancellation of Trident in the crisis of 1986. But he has the advantage over Labour's Defence Shadow of not sounding like a spokesman for lying down in front of an articulated lorry. Unlike Mr Heseltine he does not convey a lofty readiness to warm both hands before a fire of blazing public expenditure.

Owen hardly needs to calculate what will have good effect. Released from the inhibitions and untruth-telling of loyal Labour membership, set free to gambol in an open meadow of free intelligence, he does not wish (even to please the Liberals) to go back to that frail, icing-sugar citadel of unity and non-divisiveness. The importance of free speech to all the SDP Members cannot be underestimated. As Labour MPs they subscribed to and lied through their teeth about a hundred and one formulas from Crossman-Padleyism to Bishop's Stortford; Now they are risen, like Florestan's companions, from their dungeon, and they are not going back! Thinking rationally and trusting one's own judgement are not just luxuries; they are formulae for success in its own right.

Owen is as good as he is in the House partly because the gap between utterance and belief has been bridged. It gives him an advantage over those Tory Ministers who have to defend ludicrous symbolic gashes in the Aid programme, effective reductions in heating allowances for the elderly and a general switching-off of life-support machines for the sake of penny savings bone-headedly demanded in the name of equality of sacrifice. Owen has grown by liberation from the compulsory unintelligence of loyal party membership.

He has used his freedom with great astuteness. Prime Minister's Question Time hardly goes by without a polite, cool, audible query and then a lunge back. But he is scoring his heaviest points off Neil Kinnock, as, in a way, he should. Though there are only four years between them, Owen has been Minister of Health and Foreign Secretary. Kinnock was for the shortest imaginable time PPS to the Minister for Employment! But so many senior figures, former holders of office, find that experience gives them advantage only with sycophants or antiquarians. A Heath or Rippon 'Major Speech' has the irresistible catchiness of Hindemith. Their knowledge has sugared at the edges like very old jam, and their portly sense of the significance of their utterance is its own health warning. Owen, having got his experience young and being still capable of learning, matches Privy Councillor's authority with a sort of litheness. Anyway, it works. The Tories look on with a mixture of admiration and anxiety. A full-dress Party of a hundred plus led by Owen would be the beginning of real trouble.

Yet his political position has moved, like any arrow long held quivering upon its string – a very great distance once released. The terrible thing about Owen is that he is near enough to the Blue Queen in conviction to see what she gets wrong. Untroubled by the viscera-nibbling enmities of the Tory Outs, he can make cool and civil assessments of the obvious errors. For straightforward constituency reasons he has held all serious fire over the Belgrano, but on GCHQ as on Trident and on the failure to use the Government's own union law against Scargill, he has been deft and highly credible. Also he is so remarkably good-tempered, a wonderful thing in opposition, which Neil Kinnock, if permitted to be true to himself, would find out. When one Party Leader bawls, then the chap opposite feels he should bawl back; the effect is very much like two Regency duellists with large horse pistols aiming wide, satisfying honour and going back for breakfast. Nobody but the seconds is impressed.

A criticism made less often ceases to be a routine roll of opposition drums; it is precisely that, a criticism, and one requiring a rational answer, not a dead text or wooden swordsmanship. The dullness of so many Tory frontbenchers in debate make them peculiarly vulnerable to this sort of tactic. Labour throws tanks; Owen tries seduction. There is much to be said for it. In amending his style, Owen has, whether consciously or not, picked up many nuances from Shirley Williams, now sadly unfashionable (and the object of hatred on the Lunatic Right) but the patentee of sweet reasonableness as an offensive weapon. There are people whom it is a pleasure to assault in debate, others whom it seems boorish and uncalled-for ever to offer more than mild dissent. Owen has synthesized the two and come up with a brand of opposition, sharp enough and well enough researched to be feared, but so coolly put in the spirit of dispassionate enquiry as to make opponents dither and put up their dull swords . . . or, in the case of Mrs Thatcher, give the impression of handbagging a man asking for street directions.

Labour observes enviously. Of their own number, only John Cunningham, in the GLC debates, used a comparable tactic. Despite some excursions into the sacred texts of indignation, he understood the strength of soft-spoken opposition. But Labour generally, not just the Left, feels a need to get magisterial, to put on what Walter Scott called 'the big bow-wow act'. Kinnock does his village-band *crescendo*; Hattersley cries out for contributions to widows and orphans; Kaufman feels the day wasted if he neglects to bite somebody; and it is all as predictable as Choral Evensong.

Success in the Commons does not extend to success with the Liberals, at least not at their conference, where the Doctor goes down like pink gin in Libya. Left to themselves the left-wing Young Liberals would boil Owen down for glue. And, interestingly, Owen in dealing with points to the left of him is less irenic than when handling the Tories. This is an old Labour Party habit carried over into his new life. Despite his publicized friendship with Andrew Young (now Mayor of Atlanta), and a firm stand on the issue of race, Owen has no real ties with any sort of Left, Hard, Soft or Young Liberal. And he has no intention of conceding anything to a bunch of unilateralists, Greens or handwoven yoghurt-users. I suspect, expecting instant denial, that he is in his inner heart more of a subtle and responsive dry than anything else. The thought, sometimes voiced, that he would make a perfect Leader for the Tories, modifying tone and detail but preserving recent continuity, is nearer to the truth than he might care to deny minutely.

I spent a day with David Owen during the last Election. He was not of course Leader at that time, but the qualities that have so rattled opponents were in evidence. We met at Hull station. 'I have been poisoned by the BBC', he announced, referring to a fish soup served up the night before to the team of *Any Questions*. He lunched on the corner of a cream cracker and three local journalists, to whom he gave a quick press conference before setting off to stride round the post-Heath, post-Iceland remnant of Hull docks. We went next to Scunthorpe, like so many towns in Britain the former producer of something – steel in this case – and from there to Grimsby. 'Do you know,' he remarked, 'when we get to Grimsby, I'm going to break a taboo. I shall stop calling the Far Left "Marxists"; I'll call them "Communists" – that's what they are, anyway.' What he said at Grimsby I cannot say; I spent the entire time telling my own copy-takers what he had said in Hull and Scunthorpe! On we rolled to Doncaster for a street meeting, not something one would lightly do today; from there to Leeds for one successful university meeting and at about nine in the evening to Bradford for another.

What one remembers best about Owen at this time of accelerated activity is his quickness, the lack of judicious, leader-writing ambiguity. The old arrogance was not present though. The old get-out-of-my-way-or-I'll-mow-you-down scorn that sent so many Foreign Office officials to the transfer form or the window ledge has been replaced by light-hearted irony without overkill. He has not indeed done an Archibald Grosvenor and turned himself into a commonplace young man; but he has found a good humour, in that election even a levity.

The fact that the Alliance was certain to do very badly in terms of seats took a burden from him. He might perfectly well not have survived in his own Plymouth constituency. That rationed his outside travel but it liberated him from the last dreary particles of an official person. There was a touch of delicious abandon about the whole enterprise. If he was to go down he would go down saying precisely what he really thought and doing as much harm to the other side as possible. Owen has, since re-election, kept up the same high candour-to-utterance ratio. He is succeeding, not because he once was a Minister but because he has a very unministerial disposition to take up guerilla warfare. While most young men in politics, the earlier Owen included, can be a pain in the ear, with their pocket-Cicero manner and their TV-dinner opinions, Owen is managing at 46 to convey a certain lightness of heart and pleasure in the contest. The style (and the ambition) is of course that of Fortinbras. He will need a lot of domestic violence in the fifth act but, like Fortinbras, he is ready for adventures at the head of his small band.

Labour having had a fairly terminal time of it, there is no compulsion out of mere fairness to nominate someone from that Front Bench as outstanding. Fairness, I like to think, doesn't come into it. But Labour *does* have a hard man, whose ability to leave his fingerprints all over his own tractable Leader, and whose grasp of the hard essentials of power politics, make him stand out in his Party.

The fierce, pompous little Scot, Robert (Robin) Cook is still in his thirties. He likes, better than will be good for his long-term health, the title of 'brain behind Kinnock', and collects enemies the way other men go for first-day covers. He does not improve the world's love for him by remarks like, 'As you'll no doubt have noted from my article in the *Guardian* this morning. . .' He is proud, conceited, rude and extremely gifted. Cook, let loose on the EEC, has a bristling cogency that suggests that the virtues of the Scots dominie have not entirely passed from the earth. But he has all the virtues that are visibly missing in Kinnock. There is no vaporous generality here. The little carrot beard marks a sharp tempo through the dismal quadrille of our loss-and-loss account with the Community partners. He has a contemptuous authority, a dry and epigrammatical style, but he is not yet fully a success. This will come, because the talent is so large as to overcome the flair for making enemies. The mesomorphic apathy of Tory opinion has not yet grasped Cook's first-rateness.

There is another thing: Cook is left-wing enough but he is the first realist of that very young generation. He wants the engine to work. This man is not a futile spouter, and although he likes intrigue and dagger-behind-the-arras stuff to a certain degree, he is not *playing* politics. So far events have suited him wonderfully. He has a vital part of the management of Kinnock. He is in the Shadow Cabinet long before 40. He is nowhere mistaken for an overpromoted schoolboy. His parliamentary performances, though not under heavy lights, have been excellent.

Against such strengths his contempt for some of the elder men (including elder men not deserving contempt like Peter Shore) and an impression of saw-edged ruthlessness are making him an object of admiring detestation. The gap between his understanding and Kinnock's is also embarrassing, for while conferring influence, it also imparts a hint of puppet-mastery, and implies a slightly Faustian touch in their relationship. But he has an unmephistophelian impatience, a corrugated tongue and something of a temper.

However, he is mature, lucid and rational and it is very hard to underestimate his importance. One may in this world be a beneficiary of decline. His equivalent in the Conservative Party and old opponent in adolescence on Edinburgh City Council, Malcolm Rifkind, is even brighter (more of that later). But while Rifkind's entry into the Tory Cabinet is inevitable, as a member of a prospering though not overtalented Party he just had to wait and work as a subordinate junior – a candidate member of the Cabinet, while Cook was long established as a four-star Shadow. In the tenebrous condition of the Labour Party the gifted get there sooner, but there is less far to go. To revert to our sound capitalist metaphor of the Exchange floor, Cooks, although strong, are cheap at the price and will outperform the market. Indeed, although there is a large Kinnock holding in the firm, the more publicized House sometimes functions like a subsidiary.

One must sometimes make predictions in fairness to readers trying to make sense of where political power lies. For my part I see Cook as the dominant personality in the Labour Party in the medium and longer term. He may not be liked but he works. He is the perfect example of the man who by undertaking to do things finishes up with more power than was intended. He is not a future Leader of the Party, and it is doubtful if he wants to exercise power in this way. But he will be central to what the Labour Party does, how it modifies policy, handles the Conference, sells its Leader and generally tries to fight its way back. No one with a serious interest in politics would ignore him. He may have a long queue of affronted elders each lining up with a friendly axe handle. Even so, it is altogether more likely that, faults and all, conceit, prickles and ginger Van Dyke, he will be embraced as the necessary man, someone who can work backstage and speak well up front, a left-winger who can talk to the Left, but a *Realpolitiker*.

None of this will do Cook's already strutting ego any good at all and the only hedge on a hefty bet lies with his propensity to make large numbers of other people think him insufferable. But the Kinnock leadership is a self-defining vacuum discreetly calling to be filled. I just have this feeling that in five years' time Edinburgh City Council may be exactly reproduced, perhaps as Cook denounces Rifkind's first Budget. Watch this space.

By contrast with the ginger combustion of Robin Cook, John Biffen is very mild and almost emblematically English. He was not a notably forceful Minister departmentally, partly at least because he has a streak of pessimism, of not expecting wonderful new developments to be all that wonderful. The reaction of more radical juniors was a mixture of exasperation and profound affection. Affection is a very unusual quality for a politician to arouse in anybody. They are followed, as lions by hyenas, in the expectation of meat. Few sights are less pleasing then the devotion of a hopeful backbencher and his usually gushing wife to such a patron. The serf-like quality of the aspiring man, paying by flattery and rewarded with insolence, has not changed since the time of Martial.

The quirk of Biffen's popularity is that it is not the by-product of small-eyed calculation; it is a warmth won by warmth. His Thursday sessions of business questions are now looked forward to as an arena for gentle indiscretions and ironies often on the subtle side for your average MP. He put down the atrocious Nicholas Winterton, a bawling bull-featured primitive whom we must look upon as one of those little errors of judgement to which God is entitled, but put him down with perfect gentleness. The Christmas recess of 1984–5 was announced by Biffen as a short one, a trifling nineteen days. He also outlined the proposed business for the first couple of days after the recess. 'May I inform the Hon. Gentleman', said Winterton, 'that the matter he announces comes in the middle of *my* recess.' 'Well,' said Biffen, 'the Hon. Gentleman is reputed to be the master of a ruthless inner logic. If he will apply it he will see that by returning early from *his* recess he will be able to attend that debate.' No unkindness, no sneering, just the painless transfixing of the fool.

This verbal felicity, so uncommon in politicians, who try overhard to talk like ersatz technicians, goes with a personality different to the norms of both Thatcher Toryism and the Heath brand. The very model of a modern major Minister fills his mind with detail, works oppressively and punitively hard and comes out like Dickens's Serjeant Snubbin with 'the boiled-eyed look' of those who spend too long indoors doing paperwork by artificial light.

The charge made against Biffen is one of laziness. If true it is a great saving virtue. There are clever men like Norman Tebbit working too hard and any number of not very clever men striving beyond their merits. Puritan virtue *à la* Max Weber can shade into pretending to oneself that hours counted in the office, like gold coins in a bag, are a measure of utility. The imbecile and illiterate coinage 'workaholic' has bemused people and done nothing for their judgement. If, as I think, Mrs Thatcher is losing her political touch and forcing foolish petty decisions through – cuts that do nothing for the Treasury but cause significant, useless injury to those cut – the fact that she amasses work hours without thinking enough or standing far enough back from the canvas to see its perspective is directly responsible.

Biffen is intellectually on the same side as the Prime Minister, but he is both more sceptical and more fastidious. He is not the man ever in a hundred years to shout, 'Rejoice!' In consequence, as an advocate of the Government's case, he is far more persuasive than most of his colleagues, who tend to follow Mrs Thatcher in a wearing triumphalism which affronts the ear. Contrast a prim, insensitive man like Leon Brittan, for all his rosettes from the County shows, with the fine ear and modest rationality of Biffen and you begin to see what is at fault in a meritable but unsubtle Government. This does not give him affinity with such soft speakers as Francis Pym. Lazy Biffen may be, but he does understand issues and when he speaks has something to speak about. Mr Pym, with his yearnings for the Macmillanite style and for vapid orotundities in general terms inadequately grasped, always reminds me of South Dakota; 'There's no there, there!' The empty wish merely for comfortable options and for a bland, paternalistic patter is not Biffen.

He was, after all, once seen as Enoch Powell's man, and he kept close to the Star of County Down on a number of issues, including unrepentant if discreet contempt for the EEC and all its works. But Powell, despite the metal edge of his mind, is spoiled by hatreds and by a certain sclerosis of the soul. (He is rather more the thinking man's Edward Heath than it suits to say.) Biffen by contrast has no excess in him; he does not judder with rage, regarding malice only as a spectator sport to be enjoyed in a dilettantish way. For a man who was once too stressed to speak well, he has emerged as a most elegant verbal swordsman who keeps his foils wisely buttoned since he has no passion for drawing blood.

In a speech given at Brighton before the bomb, in a hall characteristically too small for the numbers that flowed into it, he argued for the substance of present policies but for a touch of Butler and Baldwin in their presentation. To a Party ridiculously dependent on the tricks of an advertising agency, which nevertheless carries out public-expenditure cuts in the best elephant-and-ceramics tradition with Mr Lawson as a notably undextrous *mahout*, such sensibility has appeal. Very quietly, without trumpetings or disloyalties, Biffen has established his right to be considered for the succession. He would not be very decisive, though he would presumably hire men to be decisive for him. He would very quickly translate his parliamentary popularity, which is bi-partisan (Labour love him), by way of TV into something more widespread. He would represent irenic politics after conviction politics. While he belongs on the dry side he does not offend the wet, still less the centre. If his physical strength can take it, he represents the perfect point of conciliation. He would not and should not be preferred to Norman Tebbit who to my mind is the uniquely gifted man of this political generation. But if the consequences of evil in Brighton in 1984 should supervene in whatever way against that natural succession, who do the Tories have – a stage patriot drowning in his own bombast, an ingratiator so oily as to make Edward Du Cann look unadorned and a former Chancellor, amiable enough in a slightly Antarctic way but liable to lose every major debate in front of his own troops in the Commons? The great strength of the *défi Biffenique*, as he would decidedly not call it, is that all the losers could live with him. The sort of political managers who want a happy party as the prelude to dealing with a contented country will see the point.

Terseness for prolixity, scepticism for zeal, doubt for certainty, a degree of weakness for excessive force, woodwind for percussion, melancholy for uplift, Elgar for Wagner, nuance for blast – it would be a fascinating substitution; and for all the men at hand he is the only one able to make precisely that change of tone. It is for a change of tone that those who watch closely Mrs Thatcher's heroine/virago performance and the clumping insensibility of her chosen political porters, most yearn for. Biffen fashions his reputation from little encounters in which character and humour rather than grand opera qualities are judged. He is a political silversmith; when iron has exhausted us and when most of the alternatives fashion their wares crudely out of brass, it is not a bad trade for a statesman.

9

Governors of Distant Provinces

Between the back benches and the cabinet there exists a limbo
of the unbaptized. It is alternatively seen as dump or reservoir
– the ranks of junior office or its shadow. No one pays it much
notice, and accordingly, most newspapers are usually
surprised by appointments, finding it difficult to believe that
someone they have not bothered to hear about should
suddenly have sprung up as a fully accredited Top Person to
be shown deference. The notorious *Times* leader that
dismissed Tebbit and Parkinson as placemen who had usurped
the seats of respected statesmen is a case in point. *The Times*
wasn't just being antiquarian. It hadn't done its homework.
But not all the middling men, the occupants of Ministries of
State or something like, are prospective Chancellors. Walls
have to be built and they are not infrequently built with
rubble.

For the make-up of a government – all the ninety-odd jobs
permitted under the act, to say nothing of those Napoleonic
errand boys, the PPSs – is only peripherally a matter of merit.
As any whip will tell you, considerations of geography and
faction will apply in the making of a properly homogenized
and sanctified parliamentary under secretary. But more of that
when we come to the whips themselves; sufficient that they
encourage a quota of modest talent to advance.

Opposition also has its middling men, though the Labour
Party is subject to flux and instability, and it would be a bad

mistake to think of ascent in that party as an uncomplicated matter of trying to do well.

The last redoubt of simple voting for the people you know about resides in the PLP annual elections and they are tightly related to slates of the factions. Other positions are in the gift of the leader variously advised by his whips and, well, by his advisers. Here the compositional role of the leader as landscape painter truly comes into its own. He must balance not only fit and unfit, union heavy and wittering academic, sense and nonsense, but also the political opposites of which his party is constituted. These are not polar but in today's Labour Party run from Novaya Zemlya to Southern Sweden. As for the Alternative Opposition, Dr Owen and the slowly recovering Mr Jenkins apart, it is almost by definition made up of middling men. The SDP in particular is a party of unconsummated Ministers of State. Looking at the three parliamentary groupings we must simply do the best we can with the material available, exactly the view of the whips in making their recommendations.

Not recommended at all among the Tories, and a perfect model of the middling man who fulfils the Peter principle – promotion one degree above his natural talent – is Timothy Raison. He is perhaps Mrs Thatcher's unvoiced comment on the efficacy of overseas aid, for which he is responsible. Raison has lost heart and, worse still, lost interest. Once promoted as something of an idealist, early involved with the journal *New Society*, he seems, on having come to the end of his own career trajectory, to have lost all purpose in life. This is a sad thing in politicians. They are an odd mixture of principle and career calculation, finding out only in adversity which is uppermost. Raison was early given the odious job of Minister of State at the Home Office in charge of sending irregular immigrants home. It may well be a necessary function and it must give a little joy to the shrivelled heart of Enoch Powell, but if you are required to send someone back, in Stan Thorne's memorable phrase, 'to sleep under a boat in the Philippines', it turns the soul to pumice. The practice of the Home Office seems to be one of strangled legal constriction. If your papers are out of order, ten years of blameless employment are of no account. I know of certain Conservatives who find any departure from this pattern shocking and immoral. It would probably be unfair to include

Raison among them, but he did the job and it has not improved him. At the same time he is peculiarly stricken by his lack of promotion. He seems preoccupied with his own sorrow. Life as Minister for Aid has its limitations but it beats living under a boat in the Philippines.

Another deporter, but a more formidable figure because of a natural streak of hardness, is David Waddington. There seemed to be a moment when Waddington, who has his patrons and is a good lawyer, was seen as a future Law Officer. He may not make the mark because of the Prime Minister's rule of discretionary death at 55 if one has not made the cabinet. In spite of having done his deporting with no evident unease, he is not dislikeable. Perhaps the natural coarseness of the Bar arms him in advance. But he is a coper, a surprisingly sharp speaker for one from the whips' office. He might have been a good Minister at Energy, where one can see him deporting Arthur Scargill, and he is at least a genuine hard man in a party given to rhetorical rather than actual toughness. He might still be worth a small bet for a place. Though it should be remembered, when speaking of Ministers of State by way of horse metaphor, that most of them will end as Mortadella.

A likely candidate for the sausage rack must be John Stanley, a man for whom glad confident morning and the murmur that Stanley was the man to watch are far past. A dull, toilsome Minister for Housing, which presents wonderful opportunities for the adept, Tory housing policy being rather popular, he extracted little personal advantage, apart from an impression of going down for the third time, like Carver Doone, in minutiae for which he had a nervous and charisma-quenching devotion. This was par for the course for a Thatcher duckling, but, moved to the Ministry of Defence, Mr Stanley emerged as a duck. The horrible mess into which the Government got itself over the *Belgrano* is partly put at his door. The only available defence for what some people see as a war crime was that the Navy committed it with the Government kept in the dark. Miserably the Ministry of Defence undertook, with Stanley much involved, to make a series of statements which, in the most refined language available, lacked credibility. Veracity was quoted below par and of course the Ministry was found out. This imbroglio was made worse by the dreadfully unwise prosecution of Mr Clive Ponting, not perhaps a match for the matter of Captain Dreyfuss, but not wise. In all of this Mr Stanley is heavily enmeshed. The statutory rallying round until a convenient later reshuffle should not deceive us. When the time comes for blame to be concentrated on one subordinate, medium-sized, lightly severable neck, Mr Stanley is your man for Tower Green – if only that were literally true. He is an atrocious, arrogant little man, pompous and spiteful beyond dreams.

A real talent, but one that has not been best displayed among the middling men, is that of Peter Lovat Fraser. As Solicitor General for Scotland in the wake of the Grimaldi act of Nicholas Fairbairn he is liable to be written off merely as a reliable minister. This is a grave underestimate. Fairbairn's anthropologically fascinating act is hard to follow. But it is not actually necessary to be Jane Goodall material to administer Scots law. Fraser is cool and wry and, when he gets the chance, funny. He has a touch of humorous detachment, more apparent away from the dispatch box; and the less than fascinating statistics of prosecutions undertaken by the Procurator Fiscal for Ecclefechan do not show him at his best. I can't prove that Fraser is good; all that is possible, perhaps at grave risk to his career, is to say, watch out for him.

Tipped last time, since promoted and still being tipped, is Malcolm Rifkind who rose in everyone's estimation by speaking in a tentatively un-Foreign Office way on his visit to Poland shortly after the murder of Father Jerzy Popieluszko when arrests and a trial seemed unthinkable. Rifkind added a touch of courage to the reputation he has always had for being clever. No man can get himself denounced for colonialism by that professionally unexcitable fellow, the Official Polish Government Spokesman, Jerzy Urban, without having said the right thing. Since the ex-poet Mr Urban is a hired acceptable face and does not copy the standard cruderies of Eastern Europe, getting him into a pique is the working equivalent of making a Saatchi executive spit on the floor.

In the House Rifkind seems to have more vocabulary to draw on than most ministers. Not a wit, not precisely elegant, he is still gratifyingly articulate. He tries harder than most not to give a Chinese meal of a speech. He has a respect for argument and a taste for reasoning out a case; he is happiest providing decent mental nutrition to his listeners rather than ladling out the prose equivalent of bean sprout and water chestnut. He has also the rare quality of failing to annoy people by his intelligence, not a problem that troubles many Ministers, but a disastrous factor for Nigel Lawson. Rifkind, despite his angularity, look of an outsize elf, and swiftness of mind, associated in others with reflex scorn for the human race, is agreeably normal.

Perhaps naively, I don't think Rifkind, in speaking out of turn in Poland, clever though he is, had simply worked out a plan to do himself good back home. There is after all so much pressure among governments to regard other governments as members of the same union. Reverence for present indicative power runs very deep in the Foreign Office, and there is an element of pure authoritarianism among certain Conservatives of my acquaintance that makes them look at the struggle of the Polish people with the fish-eyed indifference of the well-placed, taking the side that comes naturally to them. I incline to give Rifkind credit for decent impulses, not a long suit in this Government. Given his abilities – and he adds sinuous debating talent to his high intelligence – prognostications for him go very far indeed.

Quite fascinating, in a slightly repulsive way, is Ian Gow, the plump Eastbourne solicitor who advanced from being the Prime Minister's PPS to the sub-department of Housing. This man is widely believed to have been the most effective PPS on record – not a pretty thought. He would waddle either four paces behind Mrs Thatcher like a Muslim wife, or a good many ahead of her. There is a Tyneside dialect song about one Adam Buckham – .

> Oh Adam Buckham Oh, Oh Adam Buckham, oh,
> Adam gangs aboot the toon gatherin' in the news,
> If he disn't mind hisself Kitty'll mek him rue,
> Oh Adam Buckham oh, Oh Adam Buckham oh,
> With his bow legs!

As a gatherer-in of news, picker-up of information, and smoother of soldiers' brows, the bow-legged Gow had no equal. The job demanded what it got – a cost-effective creep. Gow uses glutinous servility as smallchange comment on the nearest passing citizen who might by remote contingency ever do him good. 'He will bring to bear the powers of his *massive mind*' was an observation on the defunct Lord Cockfield. He provided the Prime Minister with a wonderful combination of room service, intelligence network, ACAS and foot stool. He flatters grossly, but it is not possible in the pursuit of political advancement to flatter *too* grossly! Besides which, for a man of his character, Gow is unusually intelligent. He was indeed 'at the ear of Eve familiar toad', but in fairness, neither froth nor venom spat themselves abroad. He actually did a highly expert job and was an incomparable liaison officer. He promoted the Prime Minister less than he let things be known, less still than he perceived the prospects of distant trouble in the way of a sensible, well-brought-up, early-warning mechanism. One can't help speculating about the possible avoidance of disaster had he remained in post. His successor, Michael Alison, is everywhere damned for limp decency which, coupled with a shyness unknown to the bouncing, America-worthy Gow, leaves him standing tentatively at the door of the smoking room wondering whether to come in and bother people. Alison, despite his deep religious convictions, is one of the most inherently good men in the Commons, no qualification at all for a PPS.

Gow having disappeared, the mistakes followed like leaves in Valambrosa: GCHQ, the persecution of Clive Ponting, the Paving Bill, most of Mrs Thatcher's public appearances, and the whole style of unrelenting bombast that can characterize her when unadvised. Meanwhile Gow himself, by letting it be known (not in the least convincingly) that he would resign as Housing Minister if Heartless Nigel insisted on a parcel of unwise revenue-directed cuts in that department, did very well for himself. Gow will resign from office when Lucifer is reinstated in Heaven, but, no matter, he stopped the cuts and is able to display proudly the calluses of a successful table-hammerer. The conversion to serious politician is complete in a man earlier seen as a political pursuivant.

Promoted as far as he will go is Rhodes Boyson, mentioned in *the Senate of Lilliput* and of only brief interest here. Dr Boyson's cabaret act – whiskery retribution, and the tone of a Victorian hangman – has a certain charm for us enthusiasts. His endearing lack of charity is not diminished by quiet exclusion from real political power. Quite what the shuffle to Northern Ireland means beyond capriciousness on the part of Thatcher, who knows? But the answer is probably not very much. Essentially Boyson is a bustling, lively man and Ulster is the nearest thing to burial alive known to British politics. He will have no power, but he will make life more startling for Douglas Hurd, which cannot be altogether a bad thing. Boyson as a Member of Parliament is, by contrast, something of a portent for the future. He is one of these sedulous, Americanizing politicians who will allow their constituents no rest. It is not possible in Brent North to win third prize in a church raffle without unsolicited congratulations from the sitting Member arriving through the letterbox. There is a lot more of that sort of thing around as MPs find uses for their researchers and junior computers, and as they return feverishly from trips to Texas, determined to put their wretched electors on a data bank. It is a great improvement no doubt on the lordly disdain practised with some disaster in Richmond, Surrey (a textbook model of how to wipe out a large majority by patronizing neglect). But they go too far. The growing school of Boyson has its electorate under surveillance.

An unlucky man is Neil Macfarlane, Minister of Sport. The very existence of a sub-department so profoundly superflous to needs is an example of Mrs Thatcher's timid disinclination to undo pieces of pure Harold Wilson fantasy. The Ministry of Sport is a Cindy House if ever there was one. But agreeable though Macfarlane is, we must not linger too much over a man generally agreed to have reached his personal zenith.

We live in an age of euphemistic over-titling (also invented by Harold Wilson and ever since left unreformed by successors knowing the value of a bit of barley sugar). Civil servants and the press in their wake (as where else should they be in obedient, unquestioning England) call quite inconsiderable office-holders 'Minister', which, more than sex or mileage allowance, makes them shudder with pleasure. What those civil servants really think is worth knowing. A senior mandarin was once speaking with violent and dismissive contempt of a junior Minister. A younger and much less senior official said innocently, 'Should you talk like that about Mr FitzCretin? After all he *is* a Minister.' To which this Sir Humphrey of real life replied, with a look that would have stopped an anticyclone,

'He is a Parliamentary Under Secretary. That means he is even less important than you are.' So nobody says, 'Would you just sign that, please, Parliamentary Under Secretary?' Accordingly, we have a great many 'Ministers' – for Sport, for the Arts, if necessary, for Cocktail Onions.

However, these are underlings, whatever their destiny, and do not even qualify as middling men. One who does, though he will probably go no higher, is Alick Buchanan-Smith – 'the principled Mr Buchanan-Smith' as the *Economist* once ecstatically put it during its absurd love affair with Scottish devolution. Buchanan-Smith is cursed with features that make him look about 17. His main hope of advancement would come with a Walker government, a rather high price for any principle. Indeed, he tends to follow Walker around as groom to the stool. When Walker was at Agriculture, Buchanan-Smith was in charge of Fisheries, an almost mythical office since the Common Fisheries Policy of 'our Community Partners' finally swept away what the Icelanders had left, like some marine version of the great pestilence. When Walker slipped away from Agriculture to Energy, Buchanan-Smith trailed dutifully behind. He is one of those men set in the ways of genteel intervention. A heavy Scottish seriousness pervades everything he does. He is not actually a bad fellow though in debate he does sound as if his shoes are too tight. It is sad to see him in such company, a sort of letterhead man of scruple on Walker's stationery, but he was equipped for life to be a good subordinate, to drudge in a rather elevated way. But he is stiffly honest and much good might be done with him if, after a Walker crash, he were intelligently cannibalized like a spare camshaft.

Much admired but not quite without his detractors, is the Solicitor General, Sir Patrick Mayhew. It seemed at one time almost certain that he would make the great leap by becoming Northern Ireland Secretary. The reasons for his not going are far from clear, but it is overwhelmingly unlikely that Sir Patrick demurred, begged to continue in his less eminent job and, like George Younger, passed it up as a Belfast parcel better left in other hands. The ambition of Sir Patrick is equalled only by his huge sense of hierarchy. He is one of those examination-passing men who have other people stratified in terms of fairly important, important, very important and godlike. In him are gathered most of the defects of the Bar except intemperance. If men were judged by their haircuts Sir Patrick (slicked down and parted in a pencil line) would be damned. Somehow his middle name of Barnabas seems about right. He is, however, regarded as a legal functionary who is actually up to the job. No doubt he deserves promotion, but I have not forgotten the light in the eyes of Mr Prior's runner, Fred Silvester, when the name of Mayhew was floated for the cabinet in a television discussion. I am not sure that I would care to have that club filled by people Fred Silvester wants in it! He is also, as Solicitor-General, necessarily smudged by the succession of political or quasi-political trials that disfigured the early days of the second Thatcher Administration when the Prime Minister gave the impression of wandering in the foothills of paranoia. A Solicitor General worth his salt would not have commenced the silly Tisdall case and the self-impaling indictment of Clive Ponting. Mayhew's trouble is that his high competence far outruns his imagination; and his enormous sense of deference is a major disqualification for doing anything brave. This man once at a party reprimanded a fellow guest for speaking in terms of cheerful disagreement with a third person, saying, 'Do you appreciate that you have been speaking to a Permanent Under Secretary?' For all his accomplishments, Mayhew is a man for fetching whatever sticks are thrown.

Everywhere tipped and certainly not despised here is Kenneth Clarke, though this reputation may be slightly overdone. Clarke is Minister of Health, a genuine Minister but outside the Cabinet and number two to Norman Fowler at the DHSS. He talks well, uses few notes and has an astonishing ability just to keep on talking. There is a touch of barristerly brass in his knock-down, cocky manner. It is welcome of course among the tremulous Tory Ministers crouched behind their folders, repeating the cliché of the day as if it would ward off the evil eye. But one can't help feeling that there may be less here than the substantial amount meeting the eye. (He could, incidentally, usefully lose a stone and a half.) He does grasp essential points; he has an attacking technique, and he treats the dispatch box as a battlement, all very creditable things in such a dithering, ill-articulated Party, yet I find the Clarke-for-next-Prime-Minister-but-one-school unconvincing. His intimidating manner, straight out of middle-period Verdi, is too large a part of his reputation; and there are no subtleties. While he is in the business of being a mildly progressive Tebbit, he lacks that Minister's core of charm and his range of style. Where Tebbit can switch from cannonade to caress by way of highly responsible Secretary of State, Clarke keeps belting it out in that glassy, note-holding way of his. Equally, unlike Tebbit, he has not built up a circle of affection among those who do not agree with him. He is relying, for the final Clarke surge to greatness, upon sheer force of personality. This, at times, is just a little too reminiscent of the Prime Minister for comfort. He just might start getting on our nerves too soon for his own good. But promotion he will certainly get. He is a more substantial politician than higher-hung icons like Leon Brittan; he has appetite for politics; he bullies civil servants and generally holds downstage. But Defence or the Home Office look like his realistic objectives. The whole act is too exhausting for everyone else and a trifle repetitive for anything more elevated.

Linked with Clarke is Kenneth Baker, currently pushed as the undiscovered Polly Peck of next year's market. Baker is remembered by university contemporaries without too much affection as a young man who knew he would become Prime Minister. He has softened a little, but a small core of basalt is detectable. However, he has two great advantages: a fast-retrieval grasp of detail on dismal subjects and a current brief that looks even more difficult than it is. I write early and may be wrong, but I do not expect the GLC legislation that succeeds poor Patrick Jenkin's crucifixion kit, the Paving Bill, to have serious problems passing into law. The House of Lords, in Harold Wilson's term, has had one bite. It will not risk another. Mr Kenneth Livingstone is a superlative publicist hideously underrated last time by the Tories (chiefly by Mrs Thatcher in one of her Lady Bracknell phases), but you can plaster the buses with advertising copy on the rates only once and get the same bang. Mr Heath and Mr Roland Freeman can only once rattle their bones at their Lordships with total conviction. The Lords is ahead of this game and not at all disposed to push it to anything so tasteless as a crunch. The GLC legislation will pass. A number of London Tory Members will make whimpering noises; the Lords will enjoy a pleasant game of 'will-she, won't-she' and will make a graceful retreat. Now for this entirely predictable sequence of events the new Minister of State for the Environment, the Rt. Hon. Kenneth Baker MP, will get the credit.

To be brutal, the Tories got so much wrong last time that there is no room for anything but improvement. Baker will, however, put his technical proficiency where it can be seen. He will drop no catches; he is already coping in public debate with Mr Livingstone. And, precisely because that affable conquistador of People's Democracy was once underrated as just another council fanatic, he is now actually vested in Tory minds with the talents of Siegfried. We know and Ken Livingstone knows that this Siegfried will make his journey, not down the Rhine but across the Thames. He will put up a brave fight over the GLC but, as Mr Livingstone well knows, that Bill is going into law. Baker was switched from what is perhaps the most important of all the Ministries of State – looking after the dread little micro-mechanisms that will replace civilization – to the apparently boring and less equal job of being foreman at the Environment. Nothing could be more misleading. Patrick Jenkin having navigated himself first time against a mudbank full of crocodiles (Mr Livingstone, Mr Roland Freeman, Mr George Tremlett, and their Lordships), it became logistically impossible to sack him. Dismissal with a nice letter signed 'Margaret', as he well knows, will follow when it is politic for neck and scimitar to have a full and frank exchange of views. In the meantime Mrs Thatcher must protest her utter and devoted loyalty to dear Patrick. That is what politics is about. But when poor Jenkin, a nice man for whom I retain a morose affection, is finally despatched, the promotion of Baker to a Cabinet post becomes a smooth certainty. There is no reason to think that Mrs Thatcher greatly likes Baker – he has a little too much of the wind-up clockwork-toy politician to be precisely *liked* by anybody. But after a performance unequalled outside of English Test cricket, the lady needed a safe pair of hands. Gloved and butlerish as he is, Kenneth Baker, whose face one might expect to see above a drinks tray, is at least to be trusted not to break the replacement crystal. Once he delivers, the lady is stuck with him. Baker's promotion will be irresistible and he will, at long lingering last, move above stairs.

The obvious beneficiary from the useful Baker move to Environment is Geoffrey Pattie, a man whose previous recommendation by the present writer is sustained despite the near impossibility of a junior Defence Minister saying anything, which, bearing in mind the performance of Mr Stanley as brush-and-shovel man for the Royal Navy, is just as well. Pattie has the extreme good fortune of having got away from the tainted atmosphere of the Ministry of Defence with its grand panoramic contempt for the truth. He himself, as the Department's chief buyer, had no responsibility for whatever lies were told in the course of that long futility, the Falklands War; but the Ministry of Defence with its paranoid admirals and its Soviet-style passion for secrecy is a good place for anyone to be out of.

However, just as Pattie raised his status within that dark Department by making Minister of State, so it was broadened for him when he was given Baker's job as superintendent of fibre optics and bits of silicon. Given our impossible inferiority to the competition in high technology it is an intolerably worrying job. The spirit with which the matter of science-based industry has been approached is best summed up by a Tory politician turned financial journalist who recommended that Inmos, Britain's only stake in the field of semi-conductors, should be sold off for 30 millions to an American firm. (They were eventually sold, by way of privatization, to a Britain firm for three times that amount.) The opportunities for getting things wrong, especially with a nagging Treasury at your throat, are considerable. But it is a glamorous job in which Pattie's shrewdness and wit will flourish.

He is a little way behind such front-runners for the Cabinet as Rifkind, Baker and Clarke, but he differs from them in being an ideological Dry without complications. The combination of views and abilities is an elegant one. He has to be on everybody's list. His style, slender, bald, eyebrow-cocking, like an ironic billiard ball, is that of an escaped actor. And indeed only the emergence of somebody called Peter Cook prevented Pattie's Footlights roles at Cambridge starting a career in professional levity. He moved into advertising as the next best thing and, in due course, treated politics as something next in line, only two moves away from being funny on purpose. This talent is, however, one that he watches. The American public never forgave Adlai Stevenson for telling first-class jokes. On the other hand, Norman Tebbit, in whose camp Pattie firmly sits, has not suffered politically for his ability to make people double up even when he isn't hitting them. If Pattie can get over the lucid circumspection that contains him he could become one of those politicians we *go* to hear. So far, theatrically speaking, his timing at 49 is impeccable.

Norman Lamont should not be neglected, though, as he knows, that is just what the gods of promotion have done. Stuck at a useful job in Trade, obliged to watch the coveted Financial Secretaryship go to John Moore, he is marking time at a point too low in that neurotic, eye-scratching pyramid for his actual worth. One unsympathetic commentator reckoned that he was good for staying unsacked but without prospect of going higher. This is surely very hard. He is quick, lucid, quite amusing and politically dedicated without being intolerable about it. He worries too much but he is actually most accomplished. The grasp shown in the Regional Aid Statement, when the Opposition could have drunk hot blood, was a delicate balancing of seriously argued points of economic logic and good-humoured command. He is a low-temperature politician who does best when argument is cerebral and logical, something which makes him a linking cousin between the contented technician and the up-front showman. Lamont needs to relax, to let his lighter side develop and actually to enjoy the job he does at Trade rather more. Trade will be a stable for promotion, not exclusively to the Treasury either. As a man in the rough ideological mould of the Prime Minister and Mr Tebbit, he can be entrusted with things.

At a time when the uncompromising absolutism of the Chancellor has made unnecessary enemies over small unpopular cuts, the risk he runs is that strong loyalty to Nigel Lawson will bring on to his head a share of the enmity that Lawson himself, by candour and insensitivity, conjures up. Norman Lamont thinks of himself as a tough practical politician, but he is rather too long on implacable logic to be altogether that. He has an opportunity to put an attractive face on his convictions; such an effort rather than the style of grim dismissiveness, common among the better Economic Ministers, would be terribly wise. He has just now, like many economic Dries, a humane liberal side. There is no harm in getting credit for one's virtues, no point in being masochistically harsh.

Worth a modest mention are John Moore and John Major. Much of the fructifying talent just short of the Cabinet has about it the look of good wine from a little regarded vintage. I gather from wine-wise acquaintance that 1976 is a year to be avoided, if you go in for that sort of thing. For the Tories the years 1972–4, when Mr Heath tried to excise critics and bring on people who cared passionately about the Fanfare for Europe, Metropolitan Councils and money given away with cornflakes are not recommended. A happy child of this dread era, John Moore has done extraordinarily well to emerge as the henchman of Heartless Nigel.

He is also, on his own admission, living down a period during his long stay in the United States when he was, in the state of Illinois, a Democratic precinct captain! Adjustment from the circle of Adlai Stevenson to that of Nigel Lawson is not quite chasmal, given time and American–English differences, but it is pretty damned impressive. In spite of his ready smile, Mr Moore is liked by some people. The test of him will be how he bears up with his boss in the rough times coming. Nigel Lawson, probably the most honest man in the Cabinet and certainly the most consistent thinker there, could go badly out of fashion. Already at Energy when the Prince Regent took that Department over, Moore was brought across to the Treasury where he now sips orphans' blood from goblets of economy crystal. But this same John Moore had the art of impressing at least one intelligent former Labour Member, not too long ago, as the most candid and attractive Tory he knew. But then, I have heard loathing and contempt from Tory contemporaries. Such talent! I think we should admire Mr Moore and count our spoons at the same time.

John Major, who belongs to the uncertain vintage of 1979 (some good dry wines, excess sugar in others and plenty of phylloxera) is a good test of the fast run on the rails that a time in the whips' office affords. He is ideologically at ease with the Treasury verities; he has intelligence, some facility in public and is very much a man of his own making. Also he is an East Anglian MP (Huntingdon); and East Anglia has a good deal of weight to throw about these days as it is cut into the benefits of electronics, free money for grain farmers and non-registered ports. He is a new man for a new part of the country; as a sort of Fen Texan he is worth speculative attention.

At a different point on the Tory spectrum but also very good value, is Antony Newton. (I wish politicians would drop this low yearning to be known officially by diminutives.) Tony Newton, as he calls himself, is the right sort of Wet, not a resentful cabal-former, nor an accommodating careerist either. His first act on becoming Minister for Social Security was to end the stupid and cruel denial of funeral grants to the families of striking miners. The original decision has the authentic ring of Boyson about it. (On his appointment to the same job Dr Boyson is alleged to have said, 'A've bin put in t'charge o' t'werkhouses'.) Newton is thoroughly nice – sorry about that word – too much of a worrier, emerging as an exciting political debater. He *does* care; and his success, in contrast to men of similar views wedged on the back benches, has something to do with this obvious non-sectarian desire to be useful.

Earnest old-style Bow Groupers are out of fashion, but it is a point in the Prime Minister's (or the whips') favour that someone for whom compassion is not the wrong script inadvertently retained but a natural instinct should have been brought through. He is a full Minister outside the Cabinet, though no perceptible coat-trailing was done for him. More than any other Wet he is in fact someone whom Mrs Thatcher can promote. He will in due course become another sort of sherpa and there is no reason why he should not carry heavier baggage than he already has. His advancement has the virtue of being Mrs Thatcher's beautiful gesture.

Chris Patten by contrast, for all his gifts, may not go very far beyond base camp. For all that he writes (or used to write) parts of the Prime Minister's speeches (the better bits), Christopher Patten is identified as a tribal mini-chieftain, a probationary Ian Gilmour. He is a man for David Knox to follow, one of those William-to-Anne not-quite-Jacobites who had quite rightly given up on the impossible King James, but who stayed in discreet correspondence with the exiled Court and took no pleasure in the Act of Settlement. He is viewed rather like Harley or Sunderland and, while happy to work with the current winning side, he hardly disguises his antipathy to it. For him, unlike Harley and Sunderland, neither brilliant advancement nor shattering crashes are predicted. To take a metaphor from a different period of English history, he may labour long in low drudgery, like Lambert Simnel, who was hired as a scullion.

There are lower forms of employment though. Among those merely aspiring to middlingness, are of course the Parliamentary Private Secretaries. There are good men in such jobs for whom promotion is both possible and desirable. Ian Stewart never looked back from being in attendance upon Geoffrey Howe. With the right Minister, the job affords propinquity to events and, brutally, an armpit of patronage from which to hop higher. But nothing is so pitiful as the middle-aged MP with no identified distinction whose PPS job is both beginning and end of the line, unless of course such an appointment has the self-respect to put some value on himself and go.

James Pawsey, a perfectly pleasant but desperately humble, prideless character, was once summoned by his Minister, Dr Boyson, at a party. 'Get me a sandwich, James.' 'Oh yes, of course, Rhodes, certainly.' He came back with an expensive Swedish open roll, confected by way of transfer payment from the taxpayer to the Whitehall party-going element. (They were probably discussing the parasitism of those on welfare.) Great quantities of smoked salmon were topped up with sprigs of asparagus. The great headmaster bared his incisors. 'Na. Yu kna' a' don't like asparagus. Get it off.' 'Oh yes, Rhodes, sorry, Rhodes.' And he set to, scraping it off. 'Thaat's better, now, as a' was saying . . .'

It is one of those small but instructive episodes which lay politics naked. James Pawsey is a qualified engineer and Chairman of a company in the Midlands, though, since it deals in vending machines, the fall is less great than it might be. Rhodes Boyson was once a rather good and courageous headmaster who believed in an old and solid curriculum against the foolish and dereliction-spreading trend. Yet such is the potential for corruption of all office that the one behaves like petulant gentry and the other accepts the role of a body servant and shows less pride than the Reverend Mr Collins. It doesn't have to be like that of course. Not all Ministers are such stage cotton masters, nor all PPSs such humilitarians.

Even so, Marx was wrong. There *is* another nexus between man and man besides that of cash. Power is more than an aphrodisiac; together with public importance (not quite the same thing) it is valuable exchange! It also turns those who trade in it, and whose lives are full of aspiration and condescension, into something less estimable than they were. Dr Johnson declared himself 'a great admirer of subordination', though he had in mind a more antique ordering of mankind.

Contemporary Whitehall and Westminster are in odd flux. In certain ways the Westminster Parliament is a republic of chance and talent, made up of rogues, good men and Polyfilla. At the other end, everything which can be done to encourage the thirsty-dog look of politics is done. For politicians happily fall in love with the tables of precedence devised for them. Our middling man *in mezzo del cammin* is poised betwixt courtier and prince of the blood. He inhabits a Habsburg Court where the likes of Jim Pawsey would be buried, like the poor wife of Franz Ferdinand, Sophie Chotek, with no honour upon his coffin except the white gloves of a lady-in-waiting! While we are on to this Austro-Hungarian metaphor (and I trust I am taking my readers with me) the press is in the hands of several versions of the sympathetic and appreciative Moritz Benedikt. There is no Karl Kraus in sight.

There is, of course, Bryan Gould, humorous, academic, ex-TV producer, anti-European, annihilator of Francis Pym on television in 1979, intelligent and independent spirit. There is a world shortage of Bryan Goulds. He is not really middling at all, but as one who lost his footing in the first Thatcher Election, he has to start down the mountain. He has great disrespectful, unofficial, derisive ability. One wonders quite how he got in.

The Opposition also has its middle though it has been hit in the stomach so many times that it is decidedly queasy. The position is not so much one of aspiration as of being that necessary political bourgeoisie without which the Party would finally go into the pit. Labour Members, having so much more to fear from below, can never see the world in terms of a ladder of perfection. They have too much prospect of being pushed off it with a rope round their necks.

The unrelated surviving Morrises are admirable representatives of the middle. Alf, even in favourable circumstances, though the gentlest of souls, is not likely to advance beyond his sympathetic role as Spokesman for the disabled (which could cruelly be extended to take in his Party). But in his mid-fifties he has a lot of seniority and few enemies – the sort of man whom it is a desecration to attack. Though the sort of people currently running reselection bees are entirely capable of spraying paint on the Cenotaph. Alf Morris may have immunity through good works. He is a Labour man of an old-fashioned sort who has worked for the blind and, dispassionately, for the police, whose union he once advised. He is the sponsor of many private pieces of legislation and, though he has the charisma of pease pudding, he has probably done more to justify a Member of Parliament's existence than half the glamour stocks of Parliament put together. The Chronically Sick and Disabled Persons Act of 1970, whatever problems it encounters, remains a memorial to what the right kind of MP can get done.

It might be unjust to say that, while Alf Morris was an idealist without flair, the unrelated John Morris QC was oppositely suited, but it will suffice. John Morris, most agreeable and comfortable of company, has that little lesion of the soul that so perfectly equips a certain type of Welshman for the bar. He is the sort of senior cynic-cum-unbelieving-barrister whom it is immensely useful to have around in a crisis, which in Labour's present condition should keep him solidly occupied. (If Labour needs a lawyer at present, the clergyman and the undertaker exist in multiple form throughout the Parliamentary Party.) The merit of John Morris is his sanity and quiet lack of conviction. Good humour also is in a sellers' market in that Party.

Having gone as far as he will and having no expectations, Labour's middling man is more likely to function these days as a shoulder to cry on, a fount of soothing good advice; he is even a congregation point for mild trouble-makers fallen upon seniority. The Labour middle is not a happy place for men on their way up for the good reason that in this Party there is no up. Middling in this lopsided way is a former enemy of this writer, the startling if sometimes mistaken and unwise Andrew Faulds, who has graduated by way of various excesses of indignation to a certain uneasy standing in the Party. He is middling at least in the political sense, not through trying to straddle impossible positions but by voting his own pick-and-mix ticket. Essentially he is a Labour right-winger despite or perhaps because of his background in the theatre. (The actors' trade union, Equity, has

161

long been a sort of Catalonia 1937 – firing squads and all – which would leave no excuses for delusions about the Left.) But, perfectly honestly, Faulds has foxed the Left, who are not able to swing constituents halfway sympathetic to them against a man with such vivid sentiments on the topic of race. His hatred for Enoch Powell, which has come deliciously close to actual bodily assault, has sometimes seemed excessive, sometimes not. For all the quality of his mind, Powell has, as Friedrich von Hayek once remarked, certain other qualities missing.

Since Faulds holds his views on racial equality with such violent energy, the essential moderation and temperateness of most of his other opinions and his active antipathy to the far Left go unpunished. (He is not likely to be called moderate or temperate again for a couple of decades, certainly not by Tories, whom he has the art of enraging.) Quite why I am being so nice about the only MP ever to take me to the Press Council I cannot think, except of course as an expression of my own well-known moderation and temperate views. Faulds was, of course, however clumsily he managed things and let his anger run away with him, one of the handful of MPs with the courage to oppose the Falklands War. In the light of what we know, and should have known, the lies that were told and the truth about 368 men on board a ship killed while sailing away from the British Exclusion Zone, anyone who was against that episode looks pretty good today.

A little-noticed but important prop to Labour's middle is Brynmor John. His political career has been aborted first by events, which chopped him down as a Minister of State when power passed to the Tories and later by supersession as Shadow Defence Minister for being insufficiently accommodating to CND. He now has responsibility for Agriculture. John is among the foremost of the many able men whose career will encompass no higher responsibilities because of Labour's drift to the Left and out of sight. It is no reason for belittling him. He has a touch of bitter courage and a great deal of aptitude. His performances at the front bench, though quiet, used to contain little flecks of razor blade, and his reaction to the recent developments in the Party has been free from all illusion. The irony is that five years ago he stood (at the age of 46) precisely where the Clarkes, Lamonts, Bakers and Patties stand now. He is a very formidable man, whose grey colouring is only the habitual disguise of a fighting ship. He is a little detached now from the flotilla and it is not unthinkable that he will sail away altogether, not before firing a broadside either. That such an innately capable man should be so nearly estranged is the result not only of the far Left's influence, but of the extent to which Neil Kinnock, manipulated by Robin Cook, has accepted a defence policy which is no defence policy. On this subject, Denis Healey, for all his brilliance, has retreated into a course of false rationalization; John has not. His rejection is more important than that of better publicized figures, marking, as it does, the comprehensive unilateralization of Labour's posture. John, to be cruel, is the sort of man who would be assured of a substantial place in a Party whose views on defence were consonant with its being elected. He is also one of those few people in that Party without the gift of self-deception. Such fibrous personalities may not always be noticed when they are lost; but the effect on an organization already soft, sodden and apathetic, is to accelerate the process of not being serious.

Labour's trouble is that it has so few middling men. It has rejects, retirements and spectators, but ever fewer mid-group aspirants. In fairness the Kinnock succession and the Shadow Cabinet elections which brought on the next line of infantry has much to do with this condition. But that in turn is a product of desperation. John Cunningham fully deserved his promotion, but if he had been a Tory he would be a Minister of State down there exchanging suspicious glances with John Moore and Norman Lamont. There is a very good Front Bench, while it lasts, at Mr Kinnock's service. It has been rendered good by early exploitation of young talent leaving for the East Prussian Front at 15.

When you have discounted the men lost to the SDP, the men lost at that mass surrender of divisions, the last Election, and those taking early redundancy, not many middling men remain from what is after all a total of 206 MPs. Indeed some of their function is taken over by those elder figures – Merlyn Rees is a good example – who have decided to take the back benches seriously, to function in the Chamber and use Cabinet experience to make themselves a force. Certainly Mr Rees, wry, civil, increasingly economic with words and given to knowing a thing or two, has become a great nuisance to the Government by letting loose the deft little cross-bow shots of that minor miracle, a terse Welshman. It is a pleasure and quite instructive to hear Mr Rees these days. As a Minister he was always melancholy and slightly oppressed. Whether, as James Callaghan's closest ally and campaign manager, he had done the mental arithmetic of Labour's slide into unelectability; whether instead the successive offices of Northern Ireland and the Home Secretaryship (XX-featured jobs for any man of sensibility) weighed him down, it would be hard to say. But rarely has a man reacted, first to electoral defeat and then withdrawal from the Opposition Front Bench, with two such bounding waves of renewed enthusiasm. Politicians like to talk about the yoke of office, but five years of either the street politics of this country or the unconsummated Lebanon of our charmless neighbour would lower the spirits of Grock.

As it is, an elder generation of Labour politicians now do duty quite cheerfully for a middle not so much undistributed as undiscernible. They are like a crack regiment of the Home Guard recalled to a position just behind the Front. They will not actually be shot (except in their own constituencies) and they are no longer, in the case of Mr Rees, required to be civil about barbarians. (His comments on the not altogether nice Mr Adams, about whose past doings he has horrific expertise, will bear rereading.) He is now joined in this new function by John Silkin, very vulnerable indeed to little acts of unkindness by his constituents.

Mr Silkin has also slipped away from office with his self-respect intact, and the evident intention of enjoying himself. Ever since he fathered the idea of the politically active chief whip in the company of Mr Heath twenty years ago (some dreadful metaphor problems there – I mean, since they independently established the principle), Mr Silkin has been seen as a tentative left-winger. This is misleading, partly because the term 'left-winger' has been redefined a dozen times and shoved each time a few yards nearer to constructive unreason, partly because the element of benign cynicism, not the sort which is cruel but the sort which demurs at most illusions, is oceanic in him. His great days were spent getting the EEC right; but the tyranny of accomplished fallacy and Labour's inability to play its one unifying ace properly saddens him.

I have described elsewhere his role in the defeat of Wedgwood Benn when he functioned as a lifeboat for the Soft Left, which, in terms of Benn's patronizing candidacy, was much the same as being a fireship. This makes him a species of retired godfather, in both senses, to the leadership of Neil Kinnock, which he regards with dolorous sympathy. He is essentially a man of Harold Wilson's time, now an excessively unfashionable era for all its follies, but one which burned itself out in oversell and those astonishing hatreds which have come to us from the memoirs of Mrs Castle and Richard Crossman. Anyone who was Chief Whip to the Wilson Government is entitled to a little cynicism. The passing of time and the propinquity of the Lords makes the rational despair of Professor Oakshott ever more sympathetic.

It seems anti-climactic to write of the Alliance Parties whose middling men have aspired recently to a front view behind the railings, but they are altogether better balanced and equipped with more solid citizens than Labour. Apart from young Mr Kennedy and young Mr Hancock (the Portsmouth wonder), all who gather under the didactic wing of Dr Owen are, after a fashion, middling. We of course set apart Mr Jenkins whose underperformance in recent years is happily of a specifically medical and identifiable sort (Hashimoto's thyroiditis). He should soon be putting in unpretentious little performances that will amuse us by their presumption. Otherwise everybody else belongs in the middle – all three of them! But then what other party can put 42 per cent of its members into that promising category?

Ian Wrigglesworth, about whom I have recollections of being unjustly rough, is in fact a great restorer of political equanimity. The protégé of Bill Rodgers, always (like Hugh Dalton forty years ago) a deliberate fosterer of talent on Labour's Right, he left with him to join the SDP in 1981, but enjoyed better political fortune. That *bonne chance* took the form of Thomas Finnegan, candidate for the new Stockton South constituency, whose ordinarily thick-headed Tory right-wing position was, miraculously for Wrigglesworth, disclosed to be backed by solid National Front form, including a candidacy for that lamentable organization. None of this had been disclosed to a now grieving selection committee. It made the local papers; it made the nationals and it made Wrigglesworth. Two Jewish members of the Cabinet, Sir Keith Joseph and Nigel Lawson, very understandably declined to speak for Finnegan as scheduled; a number of Tories let it be known that it was better to lose a seat to somebody reputable than win it in the kind of company you spend five years apologizing for. The Tories, to be fair to them, do, at the top, know the gut nastiness that lurks in their lower waters, and do everything in the power of their rather autocratic rulebook to keep it down there. Wrigglesworth has, of course, never looked back. A majority of 102 is not much but it will do very satisfactorily for four and a half years, and since this was presumably a Tory high-water mark, once accomplished it will see him back the next time.

He is one of those slightly unsure people who tend to gravitate to the assuring influence of elders. He has been very close to Roy Jenkins as well as Bill Rodgers, but the mere fact of being the survivor, when Rodgers went down in third place, has put him rather sharply on his own feet. He talks now much more as his own master, not a dominant figure but a solid, pleasant, genial one who may well develop into his party's diplomat for the murky relations that exist with some Liberals some of the time. He is a soothing fellow, and a Party led by Dr Owen, who is as soothing as Sonny Liston, needs an all-Alliance cuts-and-bruises man rather extensively. He may yet develop as an on-time, male Shirley Williams.

Robert Maclennan is the great exception to the idea of the SDP being bland; he not only is a Presbyterian, he *ought* to be a Presbyterian. He emerged in the mid-seventies when the entire Labour Party, however charitably one talks about it now, was in a state of stunned acquiescence, when the first coming of Wedgie Benn looked to have solid scriptural foundation and when the most that was hoped for in those days of humble office-holding was that sense might occasionally be done by stealth. Maclennan was seen by the Far Left as quite obviously irrational, for he was willing to get up at back-bench meetings and cut out the usual weaselage of tremulous half-dissent. He is a brave man and one riven with rectitude. The scripture accepted insincerely by others were denounced by Maclennan as *Midrash*, folk tales. Had there been a dozen like him inside Labour, that party might not have split; it would have had furious rows earlier, on ground more helpful to the moderate wing. Most of the virtues of Scottish Protestantism are gathered together here, attended by a certain nervous anxiety that severely limits his effect as a speaker. But he is absolute, given to intellectual as well as personal loyalties, and splendidly straight up and down. Like all the Social Democrats, even the Election-losers, he is vastly relieved by the change of party. Remember, the Labour struggle was one-sided in terms of the malice expended. To have been on Labour's Right is to have been the object of encyclopaedic hatred. Maclennan's strength (like Owen's) is that in a way uncharacteristic of the Labour Right generally he hates back. He holds his views with the conviction of an ideologue. Given that the SDP is nationally a party of mild, thoughtful, rather unpercussive people (with more academics among them than Haydn wrote symphonies), all riding in the ratiocination wagon, somebody, and who better than Bob Maclennan, has to ride shotgun.

A milder figure is John Cartwright whose chief interest is that he retained his seat in Woolwich by being both a first-rate constituency Member and by the sort of large-scale organization that most of the SDP never had. Woolwich was always famous within Labour for the size of its local party. Notoriously the strength of the Left has resided in shell operations on parties that were run down, elderly, apathetic and small. Cartwright, a former agent, kept his local Labour Party big largely by his own efforts. When he defected, he defected from strength. Such managerial competence has rightly raised his reputation and ought to have taught his party a lesson. Incidentally, one of many points in his favour is that he beat Mrs Audrey Wise – for connoisseurs of the atrocious that puts the nation in his debt beyond dreams of repayment.

The Liberals have a problem at the middle level. They are not precisely in Labour's sort of trouble, eviscerated and wanting a bourgeois belly, but they are balanced between a very modest seniority and incomers who, as in no other party, instantly demand to be the stars. (It was surely noted, as the time-rationed Tories listened to Mr Paddy Ashdown's eleventh speech on ten topics, that he wanted to play Pyramus, Thisbe *and* the Wall.) It is impossible to dislike Mr Ashdown but it is doubtful whether, as a new Member, he actually possesses a

167

valid ticket for admission to this chapter. There is, after all, a queue of Labour incomers kept behind the barriers by a commissionaire and liable to stage a spontaneous demonstration if favour is shown to a Liberal. No, I must be firmer than Mr Speaker, who seems at times to call no one but Mr Ashdown. He and Mr Michael Meadowcroft M.Phil. (a peculiar qualification) must withdraw despite their view of themselves as chief contender and intellectual trainer respectively in the leadership contest. They are cordially invited to apply for tickets to the chapter on party conferences. Both, after all, are more important there than either can quite hope to be at Westminster.

They were able to press so close simply because the middling men in the Liberal Party do not figure prominently in Parliament. Mr Richard Holme, who for large parts of the time *is* the Liberal Party, given his essential position on the Liberal Council (and heartily does Liberal Conference hate him), is not at present directly represented at Westminster; while Pratap Chitnis functions as a mere Lord (in Soviet terms a candidate member of the Central Committee). Those who do understrap Mr Steel are either, like Mr Ross, exhausted and dispirited – sad in a nice man – or incapable of serious consideration, like Mr Wainwright. What is one to say of a Treasury Shadow who when it is explained nicely to him that his Social Security programme has been put through the IFS computer and found to be (at a bare minimum) 4 billion over on costs, acknowledges the fact, declares himself greatly concerned, and then, three days later, holds a press conference to announce the plan without a penny of amendment? This is not duplicity; it shows the adaptive and critical faculty of a morning tea maker!

Nobody of course is quite as middling as Alan Beith; he is part of the Liberal Midwest. A genuine kosher academic from a university cast amid polytechnic lecturers, he entered politics through the brothel door which leads to Berwick-upon-Tweed – the happy beneficiary of Lord Lambton's rococo private life. He is only 42 but like so many who start in politics as a prelude to doing anything else, he gives the impression of being a younger contemporary of Sir William Harcourt. He is not as dour as he looks but that leaves him plenty of room for being quite dour enough. He is sensible, not at all popular at conference – much the same thing – but despite a grim fixity of political purpose, going all the way back to Hexham Rural District Council, a school exists that thinks that the heir to David Steel may not actually make it. He is a very capable, worthwhile, grit-raking, briefcase-stuffing, committee-stuffing politician of the kind from which the middle is made. But for the want of a touch of flair, a flash of stocking-top in the big waltz, he may not excite the imagination sufficiently for the romance of leadership quite to take off.

Mr Beith might well, given the degree of shaded privateness that he invests in public life, be the creation of Miss Barbara Pym, which is fine as far as it goes, except that a larger if wholly undiscerning public is devoted to the ruggedly ludicrous heroes of Miss Cartland. This is Mr Ashdown's principal claim on the quickening pulse of the electorate. The meretricious appeal of Special Boat Services over Rural District Council, the Diplomatic Service over Newcastle University Teaching Faculty, will be formidable. To fall back on Hamlet, Beith is 'patient merit'; and while the almost offensively perfect Ashdown is far from 'unworthy', Beith is certainly taking it from him – 'spurns', 'whips', 'scorpions', 'fardels' and all.

As for the rest of the Liberals, Mr Penhaligon still does his Cornish peasant act; Mr Alton impresses as very progressive about things far away and very hard-bitten about things close to hand – Africa, for example, or Toxteth, while Mr Carlile still shudders at being mugged by militant homosexuals two conferences ago. But the Liberals with seventeen Members, though decent, well-conducted people, do all look rather excessively middling. It is as if Miss Pym had invented, not a quiet, inoffensive character with many small aggrieving tribulations, to be endured privately with a restrained desperation, but an entire political party.

10

The Barbers of Truth

Politics, let us remember, is not altogether a serious business. The attention of the electorate is kept (in so far as it can be kept at all) by performance, by entertainment. Solemn moral conflict is not what it was. What really counts is the horse-racing element. Or to improve the tone slightly by way of P. G. Wodehouse, the great curate's selling plate. Indeed our politicians have commonly looked like the star preachers of rival denominations, from the soothing and ambling Anglicanism of Mr Macmillan to the arsonical Anabaptism of Mr Arthur Scargill. The present Government represents American-inspired, brushed and buttoned-down revivalism, IBM at prayer.

Politics also have about them an element of light entertainment, like *Dallas*, the Royal Family or any other soap opera. Excessively, by the standards of our ancestors, our politicians are on public display. Politicians used not to parade before the multitude. They were objects of respect, black-overcoated persons addressed on all occasions with the prefix 'Mr'. More austere than their successors, they did not require the present Castillian incrementation of perquisites: the ministerial bone-china cup, marque of automobile and the brisk fond lackeys (of superior attainments) in attendance. Lacking wide respect, government hires it in the office and the press. Something of the old attitude survives in the sycophantic respectfulness of older journalists of the Kenneth Harris stamp. But as a general rule, despite the slender critical faculties of the press, Ministers have become a public commodity. Admittedly the condition may not be as far advanced as in the United States where the traditional self-respect of newspapers, reinforced by freedom of information acts, habituate Members of Congress and the Administration to demotic company and glaring scrutiny. American politicians are clumsily protected from the public by armies of PR advisors, private-office nodders and manipulators, and by the big feet of the least secret secret service in the Western world. British politicians are given cover by a civil-service machine, still smooth and clever, by a law of libel that would satisfy Lord Eldon and by the absence of any real trouble-making muck-raking tradition. There are at least two members of Mrs Thatcher's Cabinet whose financial dealings deserve the Ferraro–Zaccaro treatment.

Yet despite all this deft protection British politicians still have to cope with television; and so many of them don't. Instant communication has caught up with the British politician and usually left him standing. If you were Stanley Baldwin or Neville Chamberlain fifty years ago indulging only in 'a fireside chat' or an interview granted as a privilege to a reverential newspaper, you could play at being God. In circumstances of sustained exposure and enquiry, sitting up all night talking in a recalcitrant re-counted by-election, like cricket commentators caught by weather, they must play at being human. For the public this is a dangerous trend, like leaving strong magic out in the rain. Politicians are forced into a stand best defined more than 200 years ago by Dr Johnson: 'We who live to please, must please to live.' He was speaking about actors! Whatever their views on the ordering of the Economy all our politicians are in the market. The political market economy throws some up and others down. It is doubtful if Mr Kinnock would quite have made the jump he did to his party's leadership without a reputation for being good on television. By contrast, Mr Leon Brittan, Mr Selwyn Gummer and Mr Patrick Jenkin, when seen on camera, affect their own public standing like a modest round of pneumonic plague.

Television is simply enormously important. It can magnify qualities that the House of Commons has overlooked, as in the case of David Steel. It can pick up and enlarge the preposterous, as with poor Norman Stevas. It is vulnerable to professional charm – Hattersley does quite well on the thing – and it is devastating to heavy artillery without facility for manoeuvre. This is bad news for Mrs Thatcher's Government, which is up to its eyes in ponderous intelligent men without the common touch, or any touch at all. Incidentally, Mrs Thatcher gives the impression of worrying about television as much as she worries about anything. She has been into image projection on an almost American scale from day one with that deplorable, delightful fellow Gordon Reece, periodically called in, like a fashionable analyst. He is on call to tone down a vowel here, drop a couple of notes on the scale there and generally do a running maintenance job on the Thatcher personality on top of the drastic overhaul that in 1976–7 he gave to her original rather regrettable DIY job. After watching her on the first post-Election interview with Robin Day to which she had devoted the previous afternoon to rehearsing herself, Mr Reece seemed badly missed. She shouted, she queened, she did a little pigeon-spread of falsely modest pride. She was consummately awful. Yet a very similar performance *in the Commons*, in terms of elbow-wrestling and rolling on people, was widely taken as a triumph; large numbers of Conservative MPs morosely conceded that their Leader had been magnificent. The compass of the House makes it a fit place for the emotional con trick of aggressive assertion to carry, but only up to a point. At Party Conference as at the big election meeting, it is possible for a politician to be even more outrageous. The sort of actor-manager passion-tattering with which Mr Michael Foot has the infantry on their feet (the only place for infantry really) looks under camera precisely like Mr Vincent Crummles treading Shakespeare into the ground. Television demands a conversational, understated, temperate manner.

The Tories have not been in mourning for Cecil Parkinson for nothing. Almost alone in his party he had taken TV seriously, learned to avoid the dreary mantras, 'Conservatives believe that . . .' or 'There has been a 9 per cent increase in something or other under the Conservative Government.' He was the answer to a matron's prayer, not much good as a Minister, as if such things mattered, but good to look at, soothing, pleasant and nice-mannered; it is from such appeal that the Liberal Party derives its strength, and with the light behind him Parkinson looked like a Liberal. In the future a significant proportion of politicians will have to be what Americans describe as 'communicators' and exclusively so. This is not a whimsical or ironic notion. If an intelligent division of labour has some drawing wire while others cut and yet others sharpen until the optimum number of pins is produced, so must graceless men of heavy intellect be pushed into palatial alcoves to regulate money supply or reorganize Defence while the Val Doonican element go up front and smile at the customers.

It is no small wisdom in a senior politician to keep his public appearances tightly rationed. For the other attribute, not only of television but of the age, is that we use our politicians up fast and throw them away. The biggest obstacle facing Mrs Thatcher is not that her policies may be mistaken nor even that hubris has caught up with her, but that she has been around now as Prime Minister for as long as Mr Attlee. *His* popularity, if the 1951 mass vote is to be believed, actually went up at that point, but in those days only a handful of the Surrey rich had television sets. All he had to do was to suck on his pipe and govern the country. Now in the past the business of getting bored with the chap at the top resided with the House, which has its own élitist ways. The mood of the House is now reinforced by the mood of a public less in awe of its politicians and as familiar with their personalities as with those of any old drear in the Rover's Return.

Harold Wilson, arguably the first television prime minister, was so good at the medium that he fell sick in love with it. Like King John with his lampreys, Wilson died of a surfeit of autocues. Television is like sin; be sure that it will find you out. And of course not only television, just general exposure and the fact that the voters know about their politicians – as faces, voices and human styles – better than they did, and have a way of getting through them. No soap opera since Grace Archer died in that fire eleven centuries ago is complete without its regular cull. And give Mrs Thatcher credit, she is sharply and intelligently aware that the medium is dangerous, that she is not naturally good at it in the way she is good at departmental subjects. She treats television as a bomb that could go off. In a snobbish country the self-made man is suspected less for his motives than for his accent. And she belongs to a generation that, on moving up, tried to take on the colouring and habits of the natives at higher altitudes. It involved you in a degree of falseness, which makes every subsequent movement rehearsed, theatrical and, in the way of actors, nervous. In a country of social stucco she had no option. With a Kesteven accent her career wouldn't have got past a selection conference.

Today, however, the case is altered. If Mrs Thatcher had remained as she appears in that famous clip of the early seventies in which she gushingly tells a group of schoolgirls, 'No, my dears, I shall never become Prime Minister' – a posh lady talking genteelly – she would have been mocked to scorn. She was smart enough, very smart indeed, to know that yesterday's chic was garish, that she was knockable on grounds that were trifling but fatal. Despite the blunder of the Robin Day interview she has managed broadly to run her public image as if it were a boat with defective steering in need of motor, sails, oars and a rubber dinghy, not to mention Mr Reece.

There is a hint of the Adam Smith scheme for pin making in some government appointments. Political sherpas, men of great competence and the natural popular appeal of a multi-storey car park, hold many of the great offices of state. Mr Lawson and Mr Brittan are kept away from the public as far as possible, though not far enough. In the case of Nigel Lawson, his combination of arrogance, incoherence and broad-footedness call for seclusion in the style of the Elephant Man.

With presentation counting for so much, with puppet shows and shadow plays occupying the stage so extensively, all sides in politics tend to hold neurotic suspicions, a little this side of paranoia, about each other's advantages both natural and unfair. Labour, a party of easier, more fluent control in debate, is watched jealously by the Tories. Labour may talk too much but even today it talks better, winning disproportionately more of the debates, keeping an edge of aggression while for the Government the likes of Douglas Hurd talk rather as one imagines horsehair sofas would talk. It is a bit like the alleged superior talents of rough working-class boys in making progress with women while diffident and self-doubting Woosters envy from a distance. On the other hand if the working-class boy chats up with natural, street-credible ease, it is the stuttering toff who has the sports car.

The Conservatives have the press. Labour must do what tigering it can in the back of a taxi driven by Captain Maxwell. For this they have only the militant working class to blame. The number and diversity of newspapers are determined by unit costs – preponderantly by unit labour costs. The *Herald*, the *News Chronicle*, *Reynolds News* and that trade union-supported Labour paper which has been talked excitingly about for a good twenty-five years, can take consolation from the fact that in early September 1984 compositors at one national newspaper banged tin trays on the ancient presses in the antique ritual of the trade for any notable event. They were celebrating the first *weekly* cheque of £1,000; it was paid to a man for setting hot-metal type on machinery built when Asquith was Prime Minister. Money of this sort can only just be afforded by capitalists of the more durable sort; and the experience of paying out a thousand a week a head to the top end of a cannibalistic work force does little to sweeten the views of proprietors about organized labour and its political allies. Give Captain Maxwell a little longer running £20 notes through the shredder and Labour's taxi may yet drop its embracing couple in the nearest ditch.

None of which stops left-wingers from Mr Benn onwards believing themselves conspired against, and surrounded by a druidical conspiracy of enterpreneurs. *The Times* and the *Telegraph* they can take. What reduces Mr Bill Keys to snarling impotence at the TUC rostrum is the Murdoch formula, with so much appeal to the working-class, supposedly Labour-inclining citizen, of hot anatomy and right-wing populism. Populism here means not so much the actual opinions as their expression in words of one and two syllables in sentences of three and four words with regular rests in bold print. The counter-revolution is helped on its way in 144-point type set in an ocean of salacity. But since Bill Keys is personally responsible for the compositors' union, the National Graphical Association, making that first weekly grand, one can reply, 'Tu l'as voulu, Georges Dandin.'

None the less what we have is a vulgar, braying, brazen, subtly primitive press, one which echoes the newspapers imagined in that half-forgotten book *Brave New World*. Each of the five classes of chemically synthesized neo-humans, each known by letters from Greek, had its own journal; from the complex and demanding *Alpha Argus* down to the half-witted, monosyllabic and printed-on-yellow-paper *Epsilon Echo*. From the contemporary publication of the *Epsilon Echo*, Mr Murdoch has done well and Mrs Thatcher arguably has done better. Those Conservatives who feared the masses are as wrong as those Socialists who dreamed of education, enlightenment and culture. Forty years after 'The Red Flag' was sung in the Commons, the House of Lords still stands, and with it the Ritz, Buckingham Palace, the Stock Exchange, Eton and St Margaret's, Westminster. But forty years after Butler's Education Act the most popular daily paper in Britain is the *Sun*, pursued by a string of wilderness-creating tabloids whose urgent message is that poverty of mind, ignorance and the style of a fairground hustler set in type are, together with money prizes, the best way to communicate with the people.

The lessons of the wartime *Daily Mirror* were learnt to the point of overkill by the Conservative competition; though the acceleration downwards really started with full effect in the sixties while the *Mirror* itself symbolically dithered between its self-respect on the one hand and the commercial appeal of worse and less on the other. 'Mirrorscope', an intelligent attempt to run a serious, informative sub-section within a popular paper, died after a few years, a cairn on the descending hillside.

The *Daily Herald*, for all its stiffness and lack of flair, a decent, seriously intended middle-brow Labour paper, was, remember, bought up by IPC, when they owned the *Mirror*, and given a new name; but it kept vaguely in touch with the original serious purpose of the old *Herald* before failing comprehensively. The new title and goodwill was then sold . . . to an Australian.

Not entirely surprisingly Mr Murdoch is seen in Socialist circles as having built a bordello on ground only just deconsecrated. From this sequence of events the Conservative Party is able to take satisfaction of a calamitous kind. Helped by the rapacity of the print unions (a rapacity that leaves the average French peasant looking like a soft touch), they have extinguished the middle-brow radical improving press and taken most of the low (and essential) ground for themselves. Things have got grievously worse – news is held in contempt; trash rules – but they have got worse in ways entirely helpful to the Tories. A party whose politicians, even the intelligent ones, mostly communicate with the vitality of a Soviet press release now has a man in to do it for them. It is the eternal Conservative position. They lack the art of persuasion. A Churchill or a Disraeli may come along in such a major party out of actuarial necessity. (Though how much at home was either of those two for the greater part of his career with the Tories and how happy was the Party, until their grand finales, with them?) Essentially Conservatives hire advocates much as one might engage a conjuror for a children's party.

The newspapers are part of that process. The natural Conservative inclinations of the sort of money that owns a newspaper is intensified by the XX-rated movie experience of having to live with the NGA and Sogat '82. The triumph of the Epsilon press in our lifetime has made the seeding of effective Tory propaganda exceedingly easy. A spoonful of garbage makes the medicine go down. And in the process the left-wing notion of conspiracy is self-fulfilling except only for this; the Left overestimates very flatteringly the ability of the press to make opinion go where it does not want to go. The circulation figures of the *Daily Mail*, depressingly static after a decade of inspired, committed and highly motivated propaganda, speak for themselves. The *Mail* it was that printed the most horrific pictures of recent years, something to keep away from children. I mean those shots of Mrs Thatcher with her hair tied up in a headscarf (just like a typical ordinary housewife) energetically painting the ceiling of a downstairs room while her daughter looked on and held the paint pot. The *Mail* has always had Stalinist tendencies where the cult of the personality is concerned. It is as unrelaxed and attentive to political agitation and propaganda as any Trotskyite in a bedsitter. Agitation though is not quite the word. You cannot precisely agitate for the status quo, but you can soften, smooth and assuage. I think of the *Daily Mail* as the chief exponent of suavi-prop.

Yet at a time when the Tories, even with only 42 per cent of the vote, had been doing terribly well, the circulation of the *Daily Mail* stood obstinately where it did. The *Express*, whose politics remained the same, simply expanded its circulation by the subtle expedient of offering people £1,000,000, and has opened the gap between the two papers of the dubious middle rank – the *Gamma Gazettes* – wider than any editor of the *Mail* cares to see. The consequence was a frantic dive downmarket by the *Mail*, full of screeching headlines, more rape, a better focus on murder and a changed tone of voice. A shrill incantatory hector took over – a sure sign that something was wrong with circulation returns.

Now if the press were as the Left thinks, if, that is, politics were central to its function, such problems would hardly occur. If the Epsilon papers and those a little above them had made a great political impact, even at second hand through the medium of selling cut-out coupons, pictures of girls and a general preoccupation with the feather-headed topics, why should the *Mail* stick in a rut? Why for that matter should the *Mirror*, which combined radicalism with pictures of girls and feather-headed topics, have gone into a sustained decline? Putting it shortly, if sex and half-witted show-business personalities can sell Tory politics for the *Sun*, why can't a modest variant of the same mind-erasing formula sell Labour politics for the *Mirror*? Churchill detested and feared the wartime *Mirror*, not only because it stood up to him and dreamt up catchy little tunes like 'Whose finger on the trigger?', but because its stratospheric circulation seemed to be evidence of a country going leftwards – of the Left, in a style we have almost forgotten, taking the people with it.

Now the *Mirror* may have had its agonies. No paper can be directed by Cecil Harmsworth King as long as this one was and not suffer from a personality disorder. But the *Mirror* formula stopped working and the *Mirror* stopped selling so many copies. It went into *rallentando* and decline. Can this have been utterly unconnected with orthodox Labour's demoralization and the long-term fall, chronicled since 1955, of Labour's vote in the country? And is not the stasis of the *Mail* the result of the actual Conservative vote being stuck? These papers do not create voters, they write for constituencies. And just as the number of Non-conformists chapels falls every year so was the Labour vote in sustained and absolute decline and the Conservative vote almost but not quite standing pat. If the newspapers were as important as supposed by the Prime Ministers who give coloured ribbons and particles of nobility and the editors who collect them, why does the glacier move the way it does? There is no newspaper devoted to the cause of the Liberals, but since 1955 the Liberal Party has come back from the terminal ward to a vigorous interference in Mrs Thatcher's and Mr Kinnock's exclusive business. What conspiracy of the press explains that?

Even when you have made the obvious point that the heavy artillery supporting the Tories has at least held the line for them, an uncertain proposition, you are left with a press that achieves less by way of propaganda and mind-moulding than it or its excoriators like to believe. This press, which speaks to its own core of political co-religionists, for reasons of circulation increasingly preoccupies itself with quite other things. Lord Beaverbrook, that venerable monster of whom only Mr Michael Foot seems to have happy recollections, flatly proclaimed that he owned newspapers to make political propaganda. Obviously no one would say that today, but, in fairness, such a singularity of purpose might be true only of Sir David English's *Mail*.

The press clearly matters to the Conservatives. It is provision in lieu of that talent for communication which they have historically largely lacked. The drunken but ingenious Captain Shandon in Pendennis is modelled, as every schoolboy used to know, upon William McGinn who, through a haze of whisky, was for *Fraser's Magazine* and Lord Liverpool what Sir David is soberly for the *Daily Mail* and Mrs Thatcher. Whether the effect of newspapers is great or little, the Tories will always seek their alliance. In the manner of a man rich, talented but stammering, and not perhaps entirely attractive, who requires services from advocacy to that verbal valetry, public relations, the Conservative Party seeks the press.

As for the wider media, politicians must to a degree fend for themselves, hence the anxieties about television, which turns upon the talents of the man shoved up front. Now if you are dependent, in order to win arguments and persuade people, upon such men as Patrick Jenkin, Patrick Mayhew, Michael Heseltine, Leon Brittan, Lynda Chalker, all in their different ways disastrous – if not ponderous then boring, and if not boring then repulsive – if by the standards of your party you actually find the puff-and-blow boastfulness of Kenneth Clarke a great improvement upon hapless par, you will treat television with very great circumspection indeed.

Television has devalued politicians of all parties. It has thrown them back on their own merits, which is perhaps the same thing. The old unhappy assumptions of high and reasonable persons that they were not continuously accountable to the public have been replaced by an anxious preoccupation with the image. That is what Mr Tony Benn calls trivialization. But he misses two crucial points: that the public enjoys triviality, and that the mechanical facility for putting moving pictures into sitting rooms is in itself as innocently if devastatingly apolitical as the internal combustion engine, which is to say highly political in consequences but not at all in original intention. The modern politician is trapped at the bottom of a demotic well, from which no authoritarian instincts can rescue him. Not able to command, he must persuade. Naive persons saw this condition in terms of high and rational debate and, like Browning, 'Never dreamed, though right were worsted, wrong would triumph'.

Such donnish dreams, like the serious and improving purpose of the *Daily Herald*, are doomed. Television works impressionistically, often unjustly, and seems to decide for itself which god on the screen will get the congregation and the collection. It is a slightly less lethal version of gladiatorial combat. In the Coliseum a loser escaped the trident or the sword point only nominally at the will of Caesar. His survival depended on a broader popularity – on the onion breath of what used to be called 'the many-headed'. The politician in the contemporary Coliseum fears a fate even more anti-climactic than death – non-recognition. Television is however all caprice. It finds out some rogues and cranks, but it misses a number of high talents and falls with the dismal regularity of a horizontal blonde for the most astonishingly banal seducers.

The talents of David Steel, which in the cynical professional Commons are ranked roughly at the level of minister of state in one of the less taxing departments, blaze out for the viewing public at the level of a dearly loved family entertainer. He has Des O'Connor status. I am reminded of the reply regularly given by adolescent girls when asked why they liked this or that tiddlywink of a pop singer: 'Because he's so sincere,' the poor creature would reply. And certainly the politician who can convey a touch of lachrymose earnest in his pleadings will come out well. Mr Hattersley, widely seen in the trade as a swivel-bottomed and lightly idealistic operator along the length of Whitehall and Millbank, is quite respectfully rated, having always been ready with a dab of wych-hazel and a passionate plea for some high cause in the intervals spared by his hugely remunerated free-lance career. The most Whitehall gives Hat is that he may, in the manner of some women conceiving phantom pregnancies, believe just enough of his own patter to have a phantom conscience. It is all you need for television.

Seriousness also helps. We are not as intolerant as the Americans who were put into shock by the out-of-place irony of Adlai Stevenson and who judge Senator Dole to have seriously compromised his presidential ambitions by being a gratifyingly hard-edged wit. Nevertheless piety helps. It may even assist Mr Steel in his double preoccupation with holding off Dr Owen and seeing off the slightly incredible Captain Ashdown. It is early to say how Ashdown, a man absurdly dashing, as if extracted in left profile from an Action Man strip cartoon, will finally grab the public. It would be nice to think that the habit of rippling his jaw line would put them off. But, as I say, the medium and the public at the end of it are subject to caprice and not always fastidious.

Because television deals in pictures, meaning and coherence are not extravagantly important. The mere meaning of the words is no more than an accompaniment, a sort of obbligato beside the virtuoso melodic line of political style. Perhaps no one has pushed the frontiers of such high-profiled vacuum further than Senator Gary Hart, a man rejected this time but an awful warning to us all. We do not have primary elections in Britain. Leaders are chosen, by the Parliamentary Party for the Conservatives, and by a sort of constitutional marmalade (of the three-fruit sort) in the melancholy case of Labour. Yet these élites look over their shoulder at the viewer trapped between commercials.

Roy Hattersley in the constituency section, which is supposed to be somewhere to the Left of Marat, obtained 61 per cent of the vote for Deputy Leader. A desire to obtain a package that the public would actually like prevailed even in the grim salons where Constituency Annual General Meetings assemble. Similarly, among the Tories, a theory exists that, when Mrs Thatcher finally pulls out of the fight against evil, she may be replaced by Mr Heseltine who has a high meritricion factor, yet another of those Rip Kirby jaws and a manner which does not so much arrest the viewer as detain him without a warrant. 'We know he's dreadful' – is one message I receive – 'but the package is right for the public.' Personally I would take a chance on New Zealand, but the point of the image machine is made. Politicians may well go against their own better judgement in selecting a leader, the one area where they have the highest expertise. They do so in the knowledge that television has let in the people out there who don't know enough about the realities. The public sees sincerity and idealism where those watching more closely perceive parochialism, bombast and clownish cozenage. And with that misperception the politician as elector of his leader may go shrugging and murmuring along.

Once found out, however, no one comes back. And the finding out or destruction can come in curious ways, often, as Mr Benn would say, trivial ones. Harold Wilson, so brilliant at handling all aspects of press and media relations, did too much. It was far less important that he failed, after frantic efforts, to hold sterling at 2 dollars 80 cents. Wilson's fall can be linked to the overpromotion of the Prime Minister as a public figure rushing about being photographed doing things. He quite simply burned his goodwill up – like sugar or oil. There is no public personality that cannot be parodied, though some are more parodiable than others. Wilson, who has had a cruel time from commentators since his fall, damaged himself by trying too hard. I don't think that in 1967 we had the phrase 'laid back'. But it exactly described what the Prime Minister was not. Unwisely he tried to look and sound as if he were 'in control'. Nobody is very much or very long in control of anything. The politician who acknowledges as much almost certainly extends his public life.

Mrs Margaret Thatcher is in a danger not so very different from Mr Wilson's. For all that she is supposed to believe in non-intervention, fewer powers for the state, and the sound agnosticism of classical Liberalism, she is temperamentally disposed to act and to interfere. She is imperious, so not only may she attempt to push stones up hills and tell water to follow them, she is likely to be *seen* doing it. The effort made in public and expressed by way of televised and newspaper interviews exhausts reserves and creates an uneasy feeling of excess. This is someone trying too hard and spilling emotion, which we more readily accept in ourselves than in other people. The notion of crusading, of fighting a Manichaean battle, sounds to the onlooker like someone thrashing around in a measure of doubt and despair. Upbeat language carries its own customer warning. Television has been damaging to the Prime Minister certainly in the early part of her second ministry. If the impression of hyper-activity, peremptoriness and ill-advised fervour should be sustained through the lens she will set out on a course of steady political decline.

It is of course helpful to have something from which to decline. In his time as Chairman of the Conservative Party, Mr Selwyn Gummer has moved from the East Anglian plain quietly but perceptibly into the sea. (Incidentally, what's with this 'John Selwyn' business? Do we speak of 'Margaret Hilda'?) Mr Gummer was custom-designed for television to annihilate. Lank of hair, treble-voiced, ostentatiously near to God, his widely proclaimed sense of humour under house arrest, looking haplessly fifteen years younger than his age, he argues, without variation of intensity, the undiluted party line.

His intrusion into a television discussion about a hostile *Panorama* programme illustrates the ability of television to dictate its own terms – politicians go on television to denounce television, surely an absurd situation. On this occasion, faced with a thoroughly unfair and tendentious piece (relating to alleged Fascist sympathies on the Conservative Right), the circumstances demanded worldliness, ennui and a tinge of disdain at the shrill nature of the programme. What we actually got was a fox-up-trouser effect. It sounded horribly like the chairman of a student political club getting his first trip in front of a camera, and it imparted an undergraduate quality to the general doings of a powerful political party. Gummer on screen is liquid adolescence. He sounds like one of Dr Billy Graham's stewards, newly claimed for Christ and not likely to let the rest of us off lightly. A fervour intolerable in the service of God is not less so when freshly rededicated to Margaret. Those of us who take some pains not to go to Church are not best pleased when the preacher breaks into the sitting room. Equally vacuum cleaners are not best sold by a man obsessed by vacuum cleaners. A line of assuaging and distracting small talk is necessary before the pitch. Gummer alas touches nothing but the pitch and is sanctified.

His problems are almost the opposite of those which faced Mrs Geraldine Ferraro in the United States. The chances of Gummer having connections with the Mafia are not widely canvassed. Yet as television performers they both have the same technical defects, a pitch of voice too high to be taken seriously. Not for nothing did the great Gordon Reece coax Mrs Thatcher's voice down by an octave. Ferraro, quite apart from sounding (and looking) unimaginably hard and nasty, makes a high grating sound like a fingernail catching against a blackboard. By comparison, the squeak of Gummer's moral mouse is quite endearing.

In both these cases TV seems to be doing a good job. Gummer looks silly and I rather think is silly; Mrs Ferraro gives a performance that radiates qualities of hardness and selfishness, which makes one appreciate the parochial innocence of England and the tea-rose characteristics of Margaret Thatcher. That fits the record too. Staying with the Americans for a moment, since they are so much further advanced into profile-sculpting than we are, what does one make of the Ronald Reagan phenomenon? A not very clever man who comes over as not very clever; the customary gush and insincerity in which a certain sort of American appears to have taken classes, excellent timing, goodish jokes some of the time and a hint that within the husband of the atrocious Nancy a small garrison of unaffected but beleaguered niceness remains. The trick of Reagan's appeal lies in the ability of a derided character to come out with winning lines. The triumph of the President is like Samuel Johnson's view of ghostly manifestation: 'All reason is against it, all sentiment is for it.' He sounds so slight and vulnerable, so certain of being crushed even by undersized giants like Carter and Mondale, who indeed tower above him intellectually – and it is no small achievement to be towered over by Mondale – that everyone forgets the slingshots of professional timing, delivery and camera-wisdom which he carries in his back pocket.

The charm of Reagan, which he has converted into an astonishing degree of success in politics, is the notion of the loser, the derided little guy who we comfortingly know from the first reel is going to produce tricks and confound the invincible heavies. He may have no business even taking part in the contest, but we know he is going to win. In his acting days, cast so often as the hero's best friend and professional steady guy, Mr Reagan chanced not to get that sort of part, though he would have done Mr Deeds coming to town very well indeed. Only in his political career has he taken to playing the James Stewart role full-time.

But his slingshot is a degree of trickiness in TV debate – 'There you go *again*' – and a measure of polish in front of camera that allow him to be deliberately downbeat and conversational. Never mind whether one thinks Mr Reagan a dangerous extremist or not (or, as I would rank him, a rather safe extremist) what matters is that policies radically different from the accepted options have been advanced quietly, lightly and in the sort of voice that creates its own consensus as it goes along. He may have ruined sterling, but the far more intelligent Mrs Thatcher has almost everything to learn from him as a television politician.

It is not possible to stress too hard the importance of the quiet conversational manner. Much more than intelligence or being right, it helps you to win. The so-called Teflon factor, the President's ability to deflect misfortunes and mistakes like the coating of a non-stick pan, is to be found in a sustained and wise refusal to raise his voice. You can call the Soviet Union 'an evil empire' and get away with it by saying the words quietly.

When Mrs Thatcher moralizes, her friends cringe. When Mr Reagan moralizes, his opponents get angry. She sounds like a teacher in danger of losing control of the class, raising her voice to cover the want of stronger sanctions. He sounds like the affable teacher who would absolutely hate to do it but just might hit you very hard indeed. Theodore Roosevelt said all this long before TV or radio when the media meant inky men in aprons and eye-shades. 'Talk softly,' he said, 'and carry a big stick.' Those politicians who observe this wisdom, even if the stick is a pretty hypothecated item, do not regret it. It is the conversational approach, not Liberal policy for heaven's sake, that gives Mr Steel a popularity rating bobbing round and about 60 per cent. It was a quiet, soft-spoken approach that marked Mr Parkinson's conduct of the General Election. It is a constitutional inability to be either quiet *or* soft-spoken that makes poor fervent Gummer look like a milk monitor trying too hard for House points. On balance you get a better return on capital from seduction than rape. The hand-on-knee endearment-murmurer is best represented in the political context by the man who stimulates rational argument at a low, undemanding level. (You do not get girls into bed by talking about Kant.)

The potential Great Lover in the Conservative camp is Thomas King, not especially clever, not at all dominating, a man affectionately despised by many colleagues and one with a drably rugged personality. Mr King thus has everything that it takes to succeed on television. Now I am not lending succour to the Tom-King-for-Prime-Minister campaign which was always quite ludicrous. One doesn't see Tom being good at the necessary unpleasantnesses that make up so large a part of working government if it is to be any good at all. Let us stay with the world of the image. Mr King is honest, and mild, well this side of feebleness. Not particularly Exocet-like in debate, he does not arouse the deep suspicions always invested in those who are. His function would be fronting direct to camera, taking the nation into his confidence in the manner of reasonable citizen speaking to reasonable citizen.

It is quite useless to kick against images. Absurd to rant against them (even if like Mr Benn you have learnt enough of the trade yourself to rant quietly). Unless, like Graham Greene, in a recent rather nasty attempt to shock us, you believe that you would sooner live in a gulag than in California, then corrupt communications exist as the alternative to orders fearfully obeyed. Confection and packaging represent, in all the inanity they can contain, a state of affairs more civilised, more human and simply better than the circumstances where no confection or packaging is required. I am not clear what Gordon Reece could do for Mr Gromyko, but life would be nicer all round if he were needed there.

The politician as television personality is both extension and variant of what we have had at least since the Midlothian campaign and arguably since the passing of Lord Liverpool. We are all buyers in a market and of course the buyer should beware. But there are many ways of selling. The profile politics of John Kennedy have had a generation of imitators, and the comforting generalities of Mr Baldwin still make many English Conservatives regularly itch for a Baldwin figure.

The ruler in a liberal democracy, for all the glory he commands by way of planes, grandiose motor cars and those superior footmen by hand and brain furnished from the Civil Service, nevertheless has a disconcerting affinity with the modern liberal God. Belief is tenuous, and reverence not what it was. The old God got his best results and most abject believers not by doing but by being. 'Mr Gladstone exists. I know someone who saw him.' The God of Moses hardly functioned differently. But as gods are tempted by vanity or improved communications into showing themselves more often and undertaking to do more – here a mountain cleaved, there a sea divided – so do returns diminish. The god of the Health Service is briskly thanked but later blamed if that Health Service deteriorates. The giver of pensions is appreciated but is then expected to keep up with inflation-weighting. Having made his sacred person visible he is required for regular inspection on pain of fundamental doubt.

The Jews who kept God up a mountain and declined to utter His name knew what they were doing. The instincts of the Downing Street spokesman who offered silence tempered by thoughtful sheet lightning, were fundamentally sound if anachronistic. Priests of the cult must instead do what they can with the icon in the living room, the icon with real eyes and lips that move. Graven images are up for worship, but in a highly competitive market.

We now have more politics than we can quite cope with and the magic icon changes to accommodate matters that thirty years ago would have been reported laconically down column, inside page, in the later editions. The by-election, which was once an area of unspoiled public ignorance, has become a seminar with failed brakes. Background information has to be provided. So on television we get a film about the election – the Conservative candidate at a factory likely to be closed; working-class voters demanding to buy their houses; all the candidates coming on to camera with the usual stale, disregardable utterances. Then we have a time lapse so that a panel of politicians, giving us a foretaste of eternity, may fill it. Meanwhile the psephologist on screen explains the statistical possibilities of swings and, idly spinning the magazine of his computer like the gunslinger at the bottom of the saloon bar in a western, he runs through the exponential possibilities all the way to 590 seats for the Alliance at the next Election.

Gladiators used to fight not only each other but wild animals and Christians. Into which category one puts Mr Peter Snow, Professor Ivor Crewe, Sir Robin Day, Sir Alastair Burnet, Mr John Tusa and Mr Vincent Hanna, who shall say? But the presenters of news have themselves become a factor (perfectly properly) in the enactment of that news. In a non-Marxist sense they have raised our consciousness. I say non-Marxist because they have liberated within us not high historic inevitabilities but a dizzy frivolity tinged with current affairs. They have invented a new game within politics, added a new ring to the circus of the Coliseum, one in which Caesar does not preside, in which indeed he is mocked.

The media generally, not just TV, have invested time and research into by-elections, making sensations and discovering real undiscerned news. The serious end of this business lies in things that would have struck us as comically absurd fewer than ten years ago. The analysis of local-government by-elections, which were once rather less newsworthy than movements in the price of dog biscuits, has become an important if fallible source of information about the drift in public opinion that we will see realized on the great occasions every four years or so. Peter Kellner is the notable pioneer of this study; and, since it started, every ward in Norwich, Lewisham and Inverkechtie North West that mortality, serious charges or exasperation has called to the polls has gone on to the computer. Consequently we are equipped to watch the undulating fortunes of the office-holding class and make a tote of them. These drab collations of municipal voting have become the pork-belly futures of the political market.

Everything now conspires to make life hell for governments and, with the emergence of a third grouping, to make it purgatorial for the official opposition. At the time of writing the Conservative Government, despite its huge majority, trembles to promote that amiable and sardonic man, Sir Michael Havers, the Attorney General, to the woolsack. Yet Sir Michael represents Wimbledon – hectic, delirious, emotionally stressed, irresponsible Wimbledon! They fear losing a seat. On very similar grounds Labour clutches protectively at an unhappy Member convicted of making passes in a public lavatory, not because Labour is swinging, AC/DC, or even deeply tolerant. It is none of these things, but it is scared sideways of losing a piece of West Wales to a windbag in full working order in the service of the SDP, Mr Gwynoro Jones. The combination of steady by-election reporting, polls, local-government result surveys, the computer and Professor Ivor Crewe very late at night has unnerved the great parties. They have a long way to fall in by-elections and dislike doing it in public.

How far the media and the accelerated arithmetic have simply recorded things; how far, in the true sense of the baroque, they have actually moulded and shaped them, is a nice and unanswerable point. But they have added to the gaiety of nations. The safe seat is deader than God. The process, of which Orpington was an anticipatory tremor, showed again with Labour's disastrous late-sixties results at Meridan and Dudley. It rolled on by way of Workington, Ashfield and Stetchford in the mid-seventies. It took an Alliance flavour with Croydon, and now with Portsmouth South. It has become an established state of affairs which drives whips and party managers into the condition of Job. The Portsmouth South result I seem to have had almost to myself as a consequence of thinking apocalyptically and then going on holiday, thus missing the polls, which predicted a broad plain of normality and which I would have followed sedulously.

Yet, as I have tried to argue elsewhere, the attention of television and poll figures hardly does it all. Bermondsey, whose swingometer came clean off the hook, was followed by status quo Darlington. For intense local feeling, built up in respect of a well-ventilated, internal quarrel, determined the first result with the help of some sedulous hard work from the Liberal candidate; while in the second, a *visibly* inadequate candidate of the favoured new party was identified under media attention. The proper response for Mr Tony Cook's minder in Darlington by the middle of the first week would have been to contract a laryngeal complaint for him and keep up a silent movie of smiles, hand-shakes and doorstep goodwill. A dummy can be elected, even by a landslide against the major parties, but not if he insists on talking under the cruel lights.

It was Thomas Love Peacock who recounted the election to Parliament of a simian gentleman with a stooping gait and a tail called Mr Oran Haut-Ton. In a General Election he would have no problems. In by-elections not merely is the game of do-the-bosses in full flow, not merely do polls suggest that an extra 12 per cent swing would tip the whole show, but the candidate himself is under scrutiny. The electronic monster and its keep-ers may be sweeping away assured and velour-lined sanctuaries, but the good candidate of the major party, able to last under those lights, in command of his facts and running like hell, can hold the seat. Equally the nominee of the fashionable third party must at least be competent.

Ironically, recent developments may just conceivably have extended the democratic process while satisfactorily inconveniencing those placed in authority over us. For there is now a prejudice against major parties, especially the Gov-ernment party, at by-elections. What the TV computer axis does is to focus on the possibility of defeat for a comfortably placed party and to discern the remote chance of victory for an outsider. If that gap is seen to be narrowing it is quite likely to be bridged. The unthinkable starts being thought. People vote for preferences rather than expectations. In the process they change expectations. No memo has yet been issued by Mr John Cope instructing Conservative Members to stay alive during the session, intimating that failure to do so will delay, if not altogether close, prospects of promotion. But he must have felt the urge.

So the icon in the front room is a dangerous affair for politicians. Like the God that all icons purportedly represent, it giveth and taketh away. Gordon Reece may prepare a backdrop of steel-blue baize for his Leader's resolute appearance at Conference as the borazon bit of hard-cutting politics. His campaign may fail or succeed as an ad – the Ford Edsal or the Guinness Toucan. But on the same screen, preceded by earlier polls and preview programmes, come Professor Crewe and Mr

Tusa making it altogether more likely that the Conservatives will lose a seat in the Cotswolds to the SDP. Given the quivering trigger fingers of Sir Patrick Mayhew and Michael Heseltine it is a small miracle that such commentators have not yet been arrested on a charge relating to national security.

Yet we don't know how all of this affects politics. We don't know because the politicians themselves are a jump and a half behind events. In its innermost heart, if that is the word you want, British officialdom and its politicians are very profoundly illiberal. They like secrecy; they dislike the broad public. They were never happier than in the autocratic circumstances of war when opposition was absorbed or thought disreputable. They cannot distinguish between their own convenience and the interests of the people. They have face and are fearful of losing it. No more democratic than they have to be, they are peremptory but timid. They like all untruth this side of the categorical falsehood. They were caught naked and fabricating during the Falklands crisis and they became patriotic. The alliance between such people and the technicians of advertising could be a fearful one.

Yet the culture of British government is one of despair. They have more office than power. They shout more than they may command. They have an economy and outgoings that they cannot control. What survives for them is the narrow political sphere where the techniques of Schweppervescence can keep them ahead of the market. Also they are befriended by the conspiratorial and slightly crazy nature of their opponents. If British Officialdom and the British Right have a depressing look, they are blessed with enough grotesques on the street and visibly at war with them for political survival not to be difficult.

The flailing and extravagant results of by-elections should be seen as a reaction to this. More and more votes are protest votes, not for but against. This country is not very political, not especially well informed but capable of shrewdly knowing what it does not want and of staying decently cynical about what it has got. At the same time the newer media represent both a shock for the political class that has not yet worked out a way to accommodate them, and a chance of emotional reaction for the public. Like the dummy foreman at Matsushita electronics factories in Japan, whom workers are encouraged to beat up, the by-election is a chance to work off feelings against those in charge without actually doing real harm. Whether it may also be a wedge of actual liberal democratic practice; whether it will come to threaten the secrecy and defensiveness of the government cloister cannot be guessed. We do not know whether the wider coverage of political news and fuller examination of movements of opinion is a change in the climate of our times or the merest diversionary therapy.

Index